SCHOLASTIC

S0-AJA-137

THE ULTIMATE HOMEWORK BOOK

GRAMMAR, USAGE & MECHANICS

Marvin Terban

NEW YORK • TORONTO • LONDON • AUCKLAND • SYDNEY
MEXICO CITY • NEW DELHI • HONG KONG • BUENOS AIRES

Teaching *Resources*

DEDICATION

To my darling granddaughter, Summer Valentine. Even a language maven like me can't find the words to express what boundless joy you've brought into my life. Nothing compares to you, and no superlative is superlative enough. I hope you enjoy this book (once you're old enough to read and write).

Acknowledgment
Thanks to my students at Columbia Grammar and Preparatory School in New York City for always inspiring me to create challenging, but fun, language arts materials for you.

Scholastic Inc. grants teachers permission to photocopy the designated reproducible pages from this book for classroom use. No other part of this publication may be reproduced in whole or in part, or stored in a retrieval system, or transmitted in any form or by any means, electronic, mechanical, photocopying, recording, or otherwise, without written permission of the publisher. For information regarding permission, write to Scholastic Inc., 557 Broadway, New York, NY 10012.

Editor: Mela Ottaiano
Cover design by Brian LaRossa
Interior design by Melinda Belter
Interior illustrations by Mike Moran

ISBN-13: 978-0-439-93142-7
ISBN-10: 0-439-93142-8

Copyright © 2008 by Marvin Terban.
All rights reserved. Published by Scholastic Inc.
Printed in the U.S.A.

6 7 8 9 10   40   14 13 12 11

CONTENTS

INTRODUCTION

Dear Language Arts Teacher,

English is a very tricky language. What teacher doesn't know that? (I teach English and Latin, and in some ways Latin is easier to teach than English.) Some word experts think English may have as many as a million words (compare that with French, which has only about 100,000), and those words could come from as many as 100 different languages (maybe more). English is loaded with so many irregularities, exceptions to rules, and inexplicable variations that we teachers need all the help we can get. That's where this book comes in.

For more than 40 years as an elementary and middle school language arts teacher, I've been using worksheets for my students that address the many aspects of English grammar, usage, and mechanics in quick and fun ways. These worksheets have always helped reinforce the daily lessons. Sometimes I use them to introduce new lessons.

Over the years I have found that the worksheets my students most look forward to are those that focus on one specific skill per page and do it in a way that is reasonably challenging, but still fun.

In this book you'll find more than 150 activity sheets on all the essential language arts topics. There are pages on abbreviations, adjectives, adverbs, antonyms, and acronyms, and those are just the A's! Each one is appropriately challenging, but not laborious. Completing the pages requires students to use knowledge, imagination, concentration, and some dictionary, thesaurus, or online look-up skills. You'll be able to assess your students' progress in mastering their English skills by how well they do on these worksheets.

Most of the pages address the basic lessons taught in general language arts courses that fit the requirements of most state curricula. You'll find subjects like punctuation and capitalization, of course, but, there are plenty of pages of sheer fun, included for the pure delight of playing with words: rhymes, palindromes, anagrams, the sounds animals make in different languages, and so on.

Some skills, such as onomatopoeia, acronyms, and interjections, need just a few pages. Other skills, like spelling rules and synonyms/antonyms, are broader and need several pages.

There are plenty of worksheets to help your students build up their vocabularies, especially in those areas where English becomes really tricky, like homonyms and homographs. Many pages are geared toward making your students better readers and writers, like the dozen worksheets devoted to idioms. The parts of speech—the building blocks of language study—are all covered.

At the top of each page you'll see the specific skill being addressed. Each worksheet also has a catchy title to engage the interest and tickle the funny bone of your students, like "Fiddle-Faddle Words," "Who Broke These Quotes?" and "You're Weird, Verbs." The skill or concept is explained briefly under the title. You can add to the explanation or expand the lesson any way you like. Next come the directions. They are simple and straightforward. They ask the students to demonstrate that they understand the skill or concept on that sheet by performing uncomplicated tasks like circling or underlining words, filling in blank lines, or checking off boxes. All of your students know how to do that. Some worksheets will require only a few minutes to finish. Others will be more challenging.

At the end of the book, starting on page 167, you'll find a comprehensive answer key for all the exercises.

I hope these worksheets prove as helpful to you and as fun to your students as they have in my classroom for the last four decades.

Good luck and enjoy!

Marvin Terban

THE LONG AND SHORT OF IT

An abbreviation is a shortened form of a word or phrase. It's very common to use abbreviations in writing, and you see a lot of them when you read books, magazines, or newspapers.

Sometimes the abbreviation is the first few letters of a word. For example:

Adm. = Admiral   Capt. = Captain   Co. = Company

Rep. = Representative   Misc. = Miscellaneous

Sometimes an abbreviation is made up of the first letter of a word and other letters in that word. For example:

Comdr. = Commander   Pky. or Pkwy. = Parkway

Mt. = Mountain   Atty. = Attorney

DIRECTIONS

In the sentences below, circle the correct form of the abbreviation for the word in boldface. If you get stuck, use your dictionary.

1. **Doctor** (Doc. Dr.) Freedman lives on Mulberry **Drive** (Drv. Dr.).

2. His father is William Smith, so he is William Smith **Junior** (Jun. Jr.).

3. The sign said "$4.00 per **quart**" (qt. qrt.).

4. The book was written by Irwin Greenblatt, **Doctor of Philosophy** (DoP. Ph.D.).

5. The product was made by Youngman **Incorporated** (Inc. Incp.).

6. The first World Series baseball games were played in 1903, and it was the Pittsburgh Pirates **versus** (vs. vrs.) the Boston Americans. Boston won.

7. The box was just 7 **centimeters** (cm. ctm.) long, but it contained a treasure.

8. The third door is the Customer Service **Department** (Dep. Dept.).

9. **Mister** (Msr. Mr.) and **Mistress** (Msrs. Mrs.) Potter are waiting for you in the outer office.

10. In college, my sister takes every course that **Professor** (Prof. Prf.) Davis teaches.

The Ultimate Homework Book © 2008 by Marvin Terban, Scholastic Teaching Resources

PHRASE DAZE

Sometimes an abbreviation is made up of the first letters of the words in a phrase.

DIRECTIONS
Below are some common abbreviations. Put a checkmark next to the expression you think is the right meaning of each abbreviation.

1. a.m.
- ❑ after marriage
- ☑ ante meridiem ("before noon," in Latin)
- ❑ account manager

2. ASAP
- ❑ a story about pets
- ❑ Association of South American People
- ☑ as soon as possible

3. ASPCA
- ☑ American Society for the Prevention of Cruelty to Animals
- ❑ Australian Soccer Players Central Alliance
- ❑ Arctic Scientific Penguin Colony Association

4. B.A.
- ❑ Bohemian astronauts
- ☑ Beekeepers Association
- ☑ Bachelor of Arts

5. CIA
- ☑ Central Intelligence Agency
- ❑ College of Industrial Arts
- ❑ Committee of Investigative Anthropologists

6. COD
- ❑ cats or dogs
- ❑ College of Dentistry
- ☑ collect on delivery

7. FBI
- ❑ Friends of the British Isles
- ☑ Federal Bureau of Investigation
- ❑ Federated Banana Industry

8. m.p.h.
- ❑ men per household
- ❑ medications per hospital
- ☑ miles per hour

9. NBA
- ☑ National Basketball Association
- ❑ Nose Bleeders of America
- ❑ Neighborhood Betterment Alliance

10. PC
- ❑ plant conservation
- ❑ piano concert
- ☑ personal computer

11. p.m.
- ❑ paper money
- ☑ post meridiem ("after noon," in Latin)
- ❑ performing monkeys

12. P.O.
- ❑ People's Olympics
- ☑ post office
- ❑ perpetual optimists

13. R.N.
- ❑ recycled newspapers
- ❑ responsible naturalists
- ☑ registered nurse

14. RSVP
- ❑ really scary vampire parade
- ☑ Repondez s'il vous plait ("Please respond," in French)
- ☑ Regional State Voters Party

15. RV
- ☑ recreational vehicle
- ❑ Royal Valentine
- ❑ recycled vegetables

16. TLC
- ❑ Thunder/Lightning Control
- ❑ Teachers Learning Center
- ☑ tender loving care

17. VIP
- ❑ Veterinarian Institute for Pets
- ☑ very important person
- ❑ Varsity Intramural Program

The Ultimate Homework Book © 2008 by Marvin Terban, Scholastic Teaching Resources

WHAT A STATE YOU'RE IN!

An abbreviation is a shortened form of a word or phrase.

When the U.S. Postal Service was trying to think of good abbreviations for the 50 states, the easiest thing to do was to use the first two letters of the state's name. Nineteen of the 50 state abbreviations are the first two letters. But what about states that begin with the same first two letters?

DIRECTIONS

On the lines after the names of the states below, write the two-letter abbreviation for each state. The abbreviation of only one state in each group is the first two letters of that state's name. The other abbreviations could be the first and last letters, or the first letter and another letter in the state's name.

1. Which abbreviation is **AL**?   Alabama _____   Alaska _____

2. Which abbreviation is **AR**?   Arkansas _____   Arizona _____

3. Which abbreviation is **CO**?   Colorado _____   Connecticut _____

4. Which abbreviation is **MA**?   Maine _____ Maryland _____

Massachusetts _____

5. Which abbreviation is **MI**?   Michigan _____   Minnesota _____

Mississippi _____   Missouri _____

6. Which abbreviation is **NE**?   Nebraska _____   Nevada _____

GREAT STATES

Nineteen of the 50 states have abbreviations that are made of their first and second letters. The abbreviations of 12 of the states are their first letter and last letter.

DIRECTIONS

On each line below, write the two-letter abbreviation of the state using either the first and second letters or the first and last letters.

1. Alabama _AL_
2. Arkansas _Ar_
3. Connecticut _ct_
4. Florida _Fl_
5. Georgia _Ga_
6. Hawaii _Hi_
7. Idaho _Id_
8. Illinois _IL_
9. Indiana _In_
10. Iowa _Ia_

11. Kansas _Kn_
12. Kentucky _Ky_
13. Louisiana _La_
14. Maine _Maa_
15. Maryland _Md_
16. Massachusetts _MS_
17. Michigan _mi_
18. Nebraska _Nb_
19. Ohio _oh_
20. Oklahoma _Ok_

21. Oregon _OR_
22. Pennsylvania _Pn_
23. Utah _ut_
24. Vermont _VM_
25. Virginia _vi_
26. Washington _wa_
27. Wisconsin _Wi_
28. Wyoming _wy_

★ ★ ★ ★ ★ ★ ★ ★

The abbreviations of three states are the same if you use

● the first two letters

● the first and last letters

Write the names of these three states along with their abbreviations.

_____

_____

_____

The Ultimate Homework Book © 2008 by Marvin Terban, Scholastic Teaching Resources

Challenge

GET YOUR STATES STRAIGHT

Many of the 50 states have abbreviations that are made of their first and last letters or their first and second letters.

States with two words in their names are always abbreviated with the first letter of each word.

All the other states are abbreviated with their first letter and another letter in the name.

DIRECTIONS
On each line below, write the two-letter abbreviations of the states.

1. Alaska _____

2. Arizona _____

3. Minnesota _____

4. Mississippi _____

5. Missouri _____

6. Montana _____

7. Nevada _____

8. New Hampshire _____

9. New Jersey _____

10. New Mexico _____

11. New York _____

12. North Carolina _____

13. North Dakota _____

14. Rhode Island _____

15. South Carolina _____

16. South Dakota _____

17. Tennessee _____

18. Texas _____

19. West Virginia _____

The Ultimate Homework Book © 2008 by Marvin Terban, Scholastic Teaching Resources

DEPARTMENT OF STATES

Some of the state abbreviations also make real two-letter words.

DIRECTIONS

Using the definitions in the first column below, fill in the second column with a two-letter word that fits the definition. Fill in the third column with the name of the state whose abbreviation is the same as that two-letter word.

Definition	Abbreviation	Name of State
A word expressing mild surprise	OH	Ohio

Definition	Abbreviation	Name of State
1. A friendly greeting	Hi	Hawaii
2. The opposite of "out"	in	indiana
3. Myself	me	maine
4. Medical doctor	md	maryland
5. Mother (informal)	mck	massachusets
6. Father (informal)	pa	pennsylvania
7. A conjunction	OR	oregon
8. All right, fine, good	OK	okhlana
9. The note after *do* and *re*	mi	michigan
10. The note after *so*	La	louisiana

The Ultimate Homework Book © 2008 by Marvin Terban, Scholastic Teaching Resources

STATES CAN TALK

If you write out the abbreviations of some states in a row, you can make little sentences.

DIRECTIONS
Fill in the blank lines below to make sentences out of state abbreviations.

1. A way of greeting your mother and your father.

   Hawaii, Massachusetts. Hawaii, Pennsylvania.

   HI , MA . HI , PA .

2. Either your mother or your father.

   Massachusetts Oregon Pennsylvania.

   MA OR PA .

3. How Tarzan would reply if you asked him if he was all right.

   Maine Oklahoma.

   ME OK .

4. Doctor mother.

   Maryland Massachusetts.

   MD . MA .

5. Where's all the pie Ma baked?

   Indiana Pennsylvania

   IN PA .

The Ultimate Homework Book © 2008 by Marvin Terban, Scholastic Teaching Resources

STATE YOUR WORDS

If you combine the abbreviations of two states, you can sometimes get a real word.

DIRECTIONS

Fill in the blank boxes in each row below with words that match the definitions and the names of states whose combined abbreviations make those words. The first one has been done for you.

Definition	Is the word	Made from the abbreviation for the state of	Plus the abbreviation for the state of
1. Black rock used as fuel	COAL	Colorado	Alabama
2. Keep out of sight			
3. Hair on neck of lion			
4. Country road			
5. Breakfast, lunch, or dinner			
6. Got your money			
7. Back legs of horse			
8. Heath, open land			
9. Physical suffering			
10. Walking stick			
11. Fix, repair			
12. Travel on horse, bike, etc.			
13. Secret writing			
14. Earth, ground			
15. Tells which way the wind is blowing			
16. Outer skin of fruit			

The Ultimate Homework Book © 2008 by Marvin Terban, Scholastic Teaching Resources

WORDS FROM INITIALS

Have you ever wondered what "radar" or "zip" (as in "zip code") means? These words are acronyms. An acronym is a word usually made up of the first letters of other words.

DIRECTIONS
Match the acronym to its full meaning by writing the numbers of the correct acronyms on the blank lines in front of the meanings.

ACRONYMS

1. _____ AIDS
2. _____ AWOL
3. _____ CORE
4. _____ FAQS
5. _____ JPEG
6. _____ LASER
7. _____ MADD
8. _____ NASA
9. _____ NATO
10. _____ NIMBY
11. _____ OPEC
12. _____ RADAR
13. _____ ROM
14. _____ SADD
15. _____ SCUBA
16. _____ SONAR
17. _____ SWAK
18. _____ UNESCO
19. _____ ZIP

MEANINGS

a. Sound navigation ranging

b. Not in my backyard

c. Acquired Immune Deficiency Syndrome

d. Joint Photographic Experts Group

e. Absent without official leave

f. Zone improvement plan

g. Light amplification by stimulated emission of radiation

h. Mothers Against Drunk Driving

i. Sealed with a kiss

j. Congress of Racial Equality

k. National Aeronautics and Space Administration

l. Read-only memory

m. Radio detecting and ranging

n. Organization of Petroleum Exporting Countries

o. North Atlantic Treaty Organization

p. Self-contained Underwater Breathing Apparatus

q. United Nations Educational, Scientific, and Cultural Organization

r. Students Against Destructive Decisions

s. Frequently asked questions

The Ultimate Homework Book © 2008 by Marvin Terban, Scholastic Teaching Resources

FAFA: FIND ALL FAKE ACRONYMS

An acronym is a word usually made up of the first letters of other words. There are thousands of acronyms in English. Some are common, like PIN (Personal Identification Number). Some are not so common, like CAV (Constant Air Volume).

DIRECTION

Below is a list of 30 acronyms. Most of them are real. But a few are totally fake. Can you tell the difference? On the blank line in front of each acronym, print **R** if you think it's real, **F** if you think it's fake. Using an Internet search engine might help you decide.

1. _____ **ASHCAT** Association of Safety & Health Consultants and Trainers Inc.
2. _____ **BARF** Bureau of Animal Research and Feathers
3. _____ **BAT** Best Available Technology
4. _____ **DODO** Department of Dead Ostriches
5. _____ **DOT** Department of Transportation
6. _____ **FEMA** Federal Emergency Management Agency
7. _____ **FIFRA** Federal Insecticide, Fungicide, and Rodenticide Act
8. _____ **FIP** Final Implementation Plan
9. _____ **GERT** General Employee Radiological Training
10. _____ **GROSS** Grand Royal Octopus Scientific Society
11. _____ **HAZMAT** Hazardous Materials
12. _____ **HAZWOPER** Hazardous Waste Operations Emergency Response
13. _____ **IHIT** Industrial Hygienist in Training
14. _____ **LALA** League of American Lollipop Advocates
15. _____ **LED** Light-Emitting Diode
16. _____ **LUFT** Leaking Underground Fuel Tank
17. _____ **ORP** Oxidation Reduction Potential
18. _____ **OSHA** Occupational Safety & Health Administration
19. _____ **PAPR** Powered Air-Purifying Respirator
20. _____ **PIKL** Professional Insect and Kangaroo Lovers
21. _____ **POP** Performance-Oriented Packaging
22. _____ **RAP** Remedial Action Plan
23. _____ **SARA** Superfund Amendments and Reauthorization Act
24. _____ **SHEP** Safety, Health, and Environmental Program
25. _____ **SOP** Standard Operating Procedures
26. _____ **VAV** Variable Air Volume
27. _____ **WAFFLE** World Association of the Fuzzy Fungus Lunar Environment
28. _____ **WEEL** Workplace Environmental Exposure Limit
29. _____ **WHO** World Health Organization
30. _____ **YUKKY** Youthful Union of Kindergarten Kid Yodelers

The Ultimate Homework Book © 2008 by Marvin Terban, Scholastic Teaching Resources

TALLER THAN TALL

Tim is tall, but his uncle is even taller. **Tall** and **taller** are adjectives (words that describe nouns). **Tall** is a regular adjective, which is called the positive degree. **Taller** is the comparative degree of the adjective. We use it to compare two people, places, or things.

We add **-er** to most one- and two-syllable adjectives to make them comparative. If the word ends with **-y**, remember to change the **y** to **i** before adding **-er**.

When an adjective is longer, three syllables or more, we put **more** in front of it. For example:

> The Colossus of Rhodes was a **beautiful** statue, but I think the Statue of Liberty is even **more beautiful**.

DIRECTIONS

On the blank lines in the sentences below, write the comparative degrees of the adjectives in boldface. If you're not sure of the spelling, check your dictionary. Sometimes you just have to add **-er**, and sometimes you have to put **more** in front of the adjective.

1. My cousin thinks she's so **smart**, but I am a _____ person by far, and not conceited about it, either.

2. Since your **glamorous** gown was eaten by the dragon, Princess, the royal tailors have made you an even _____ gown.

3. If you think a baby elephant is a **heavy** thing to carry, try lifting this baby hippo; it's much _____ .

4. My grandma always baked **mouthwatering** cakes, but now that she's graduated from pastry school, her cakes are _____ .

5. Your mother said your room was **messy**, but if she ever saw my room, she'd know that mine is _____ than yours by a long shot!

6. The movie we saw last week was **funny**, but the one we saw tonight was _____ by a thousand laughs.

7. He thinks that the Haunted House ride is **frightening**, but the Tower of Snakes ride is much _____ .

8. Okay, King Kong was **colossal**, but don't you think that Godzilla was _____ by at least a few inches?

The Ultimate Homework Book © 2008 by Marvin Terban, Scholastic Teaching Resources

TO THE MAX!

The superlative degree of an adjective is used to compare three or more persons, places, or things. If the adjective is short, one- or two-syllables long, just add **-est** to form the superlative degree. For example:

> Darren is a **great** (positive degree) singer.
>
> Ryan is even **greater** (comparative degree).
>
> But Sam is the **greatest** (superlative degree) singer ever.

If the word ends with **-y**, remember to change the **y** to **i** before adding **-est**.

If the adjective is three syllables long or longer, put **most** in front of it. For example:

> The chocolate cake is **delicious** (positive degree), but that pecan pie is even **more delicious** (comparative degree), and this cherry cheesecake is the **most delicious** (superlative degree) dessert ever created!

DIRECTIONS

On the blank lines in the sentences below, write the superlative degrees of the adjectives in boldface. If you're not sure of the spelling, check your dictionary. Is it **-est** at the end or **most** at the beginning?

1. A rose is a **pretty** flower, but I think that the tulips are the _____ flowers in my garden.

2. The Amazon may be a **long** river, but the _____ river in the world is the Nile.

3. I thought my bed at home was **soft** until I fell asleep on the _____ mattress imaginable, at the Sweet Slumber Hotel.

4. Your Doberman pinscher may be big, but he isn't so **ferocious**. My little Chihuahua is the _____ dog who ever barked.

5. Getting the leading role was a **happy** day for me, but getting a standing ovation was definitely the _____ experience of my life.

6. Your little brother is an **intelligent** kid, I agree, but he isn't the _____ human being ever born.

7. Class, as everyone knows, sugar is **sweet**, but the _____ substance on the planet, thaumatin, comes from a plant in Africa called the katemfe fruit.

8. Diving into a bucket of water from a height of 100 feet is an **amazing** stunt, but doing it covered in jelly is the _____ stunt I ever saw.

22

The Ultimate Homework Book © 2008 by Marvin Terban, Scholastic Teaching Resources

WEIRD ADJECTIVES

If all adjectives just called for adding **-er** and **-est** or **more** and **most**, English grammar would be a lot easier. But, alas, some adjectives are **irregular**, or not normal, and they form their comparative and superlative degrees in weird ways, like changing into totally new words.

DIRECTIONS
On the blank lines in the sentences below, write the comparative and superlative degrees of the adjectives in boldface. Careful. Some of them are really tricky. Keep a good dictionary nearby.

1. A gerbil is a **good** pet, but I think a tarantula is a _____ pet for little kids, and, no doubt about it, an alligator is the _____ pet a kid could have.

2. I got a **bad** grade on the math test, but my science grade was even _____ , and it still wasn't as bad as my history grade, which was the _____ grade I ever got in my entire life.

3. **Many** people live in New York City, but even _____ live in Shanghai in China, and the city with the _____ people is Mumbai (Bombay) in India.

4. This sphynx cat has very **little** hair, but that one has even _____ , and this one has the _____ amount of hair of any cat in this litter.

5. **Some** snow fell today, _____ is expected tomorrow, and by Thursday the _____ snow ever recorded will have fallen on our little town.

The Ultimate Homework Book © 2008 by Marvin Terban, Scholastic Teaching Resources

DESCRIBE THE OCTOPUS THAT HUGGED YOU

Animals are so much a part of our world that many words in the English language relate to them. For example, if someone in a story you're writing moves like a cat, you can describe him or her as being "feline." If you read in a book that a character is "simian," that means he or she looks or acts like a monkey.

DIRECTIONS
Match the animals to their adjectives. From the words in the box below, choose words to fit into the blank spaces. You might be able to guess some of these words, but many will be new to you, so get your dictionary ready.

bovine	bubaline	cameline	canine	crocodilian	delphine	elephantine
equine	galline	giraffine	hominine	lionine	octopine	piscine
procine	ranine	reptilian	serpentine	taurine	ursine	vulpine

ANIMAL	ANIMAL ADJECTIVE	ANIMAL	ANIMAL ADJECTIVE
1. bear	_____	**11.** fish	_____
2. buffalo	_____	**12.** fox	_____
3. bull	_____	**13.** frog	_____
4. camel	_____	**14.** giraffe	_____
5. chicken	_____	**15.** horse	_____
6. cow	_____	**16.** lion	_____
7. crocodile	_____	**17.** octopus	_____
8. dog	_____	**18.** pig	_____
9. dolphin	_____	**19.** reptile	_____
10. elephant	_____	**20.** serpent	_____

★ ★ ★ ★ ★ ★ ★ ★

What does the leftover adjective describe?

The Ultimate Homework Book © 2008 by Marvin Terban, Scholastic Teaching Resources

SAY IT PROPERLY

A proper noun is the name of a specific person, place, or thing, and always begins with a capital letter. For example:

> George Washington, Chicago, Apple computers

A proper adjective comes from a proper noun. For example:

> Plays written by Shakespeare are **Shakespearean**.

> Something made in Italy is **Italian**.

DIRECTIONS

In the sentences below, change the proper nouns in boldface into proper adjectives. Careful! Some are tricky.

1. When I go to **France**, I will eat a big, long roll of delicious _____ bread.

2. **China** is the most heavily populated nation on Earth because over one billion _____ people live there.

3. People who live in **Australia** speak English, but it's a very _____ kind of English.

4. I never understood why _____ cheese had so many holes in it, so I took a trip to **Switzerland** to find out.

5. The time that Queen **Victoria** ruled Great Britain in the 1800s is now called the _____ Age.

6. I wonder if _____ jumping beans really come from **Mexico**.

7. Since Shakespeare wrote his sonnets when **Elizabeth I** was queen of England, they're called _____ sonnets.

8. I'm reading a new book about the planet **Mars** because I love anything _____ .

9. This little store sells folk art from **Peru**, and I just love _____ ceramics.

10. The new chef in my cousin's restaurant comes from **Ireland** and can cook a fabulous _____ stew.

The Ultimate Homework Book © 2008 by Marvin Terban, Scholastic Teaching Resources

WHAT'S A NICE -LY LIKE YOU DOING ON AN ADJECTIVE LIKE THAT?

Many adverbs end with **-ly** and answer the question "how?" about a verb. For example:

> The baby hippo looked lovingly at its mother.

How did it look? Lovingly. **Lovingly** is the adverb.

But not all words that end with **-ly** are adverbs. Some are adjectives (words that describe nouns). Adjectives often answer the question "what kind of?" about a noun. For example:

> My brother is a silly kid.

Silly ends with **-ly**, but it's not an adverb. It's an adjective because it describes a kid (a noun) and tells what kind of a kid he is. He's silly.

DIRECTIONS

In the newspaper headlines below, all the words in boldface end with **-ly**. Some of the words are adverbs. The others are adjectives. Above each boldface word print **ADJ.** if it's an adjective or **ADV.** if it's an adverb. Remember, in these headlines, if the word is describing a noun and answering the question "what kind of?" it's an adjective. If the word is describing a verb and answering the question "how?" it's an adverb. Careful. This can be tricky.

1. **CHILLY** DAY SPOILS FOURTH OF JULY PARADE

2. COUPLE IS **HAPPILY** MARRIED FOR 75 YEARS

3. CITIZENS DEMAND CLEANUP OF **SMELLY** DUMP

4. MAYOR **LOUDLY** DEMANDS A RECOUNT OF VOTES

5. **ELDERLY** MAN CLIMBS WORLD'S HIGHEST MOUNTAIN

6. AMAZING FACE CREAM MAKES **UGLY** GORILLA PRETTY

7. LOTTERY WINNER **FOOLISHLY** LOSES WINNING TICKET

8. GIRL WITH **CURLY** HAIR CLIMBS TREE TO RESCUE CAT

9. BOY **BOLDLY** SAVES TOWN FROM HICCUPPING DISEASE

10. QUEEN'S DOG GIVES BIRTH TO **CUDDLY** PUPPIES

The Ultimate Homework Book © 2008 by Marvin Terban, Scholastic Teaching Resources

AMAZINGLY EASILY!

An adjective is a word that describes a noun (the name of a person, place, thing, or idea).

An adverb is a word that describes a verb (an action word). You can change many (but not all) adjectives into adverbs by adding **-ly** to the end of the word.

DIRECTIONS

In the sentences below, the same word appears twice in boldface. One of these words is an adjective describing a noun. One is an adverb describing a verb. But the adverb is missing its **-ly** ending. Add **-ly** to one of the words in each sentence to turn it into an adverb. Leave the other word alone.

1. The amazingly **swift**   runner ran **swift**   toward the finish line.

2. Karen told the **beautiful**   story **beautiful**   to the fascinated children.

3. "I told you the truth **honest**   ," said the man to the police officer, "because I am an **honest**   man."

4. "Send the **quick**   messenger to deliver the message **quick**   to the king!" shouted the general.

5. With his incredibly **loud**   voice, the president spoke **loud**   to the huge crowd in the square.

6. "The doctor will see you **short**   ," said the nurse with the **short**   haircut.

7. Grandma stroked the crying girl's face **soft**   with her **soft**   hands.

8. As she ate one of the **sweet**   rolls, she began singing **sweet**   to herself.

9. The opera singer's voice was in **bad**   shape, so he sang **bad**   that night.

10. The old man with the long beard spoke very **wise**   to the magician and gave him some **wise**   advice.

The Ultimate Homework Book © 2008 by Marvin Terban, Scholastic Teaching Resources

POOF! YOU'RE AN ADVERB!

Sometimes when you change an adjective into an adverb, you have to change the spelling a little before you add **-ly**. For instance, **happy** becomes **happily** and **terrible** becomes **terribly**. Sometimes the adjective and the adverb are the same word. For example:

The **early** bird always wakes up **early** in the morning.

Sometimes the adjective changes into a completely different word. Yikes! Adjectives and adverbs are tricky.

DIRECTIONS

In the sentences below, there is an adjective in boldface and a blank line. On the blank line in each sentence, neatly write the adverb form of the adjective in boldface. Check your spelling in a dictionary if you're not sure.

1. It was a very **noisy** birthday party, and everyone sang and danced _____ until the neighbors complained.

2. He had an extremely **hard** job, but the coal miner worked _____ at it every day.

3. The queen wanted the palace to be **tidy**, so the dutiful maid cleaned all 146 rooms _____ every day.

4. I chose a large, **fast** horse and rode to the village as _____ as I could.

5. The **hungry** street urchin stared _____ into the bakery shop window.

6. My uncle made a **hasty** decision and ran _____ out of the zoo when he saw the kangaroo hopping toward him.

7. If you want to be known as a **good** cook, you'll have to learn how to cook _____ .

8. We joked that she would be **late** to her own wedding, and she actually did arrive _____ to the ceremony!

9. Your sister is a **sensible** person and she will advise you _____ about this matter.

10. I knew Mr. Williams was **angry** that I had broken the window when he stopped smiling and started shouting _____ at me.

The Ultimate Homework Book © 2008 by Marvin Terban, Scholastic Teaching Resources

HOW DO THEY DO THAT?

Adverbs are extremely useful words. Many adverbs describe verbs (words that show action) and answer the question "how?" For example:

    The chicken played the piano beautifully.

How did the chicken play? Beautifully. **Beautifully** is the adverb.

Many, but not all, adverbs end with **-ly**.

DIRECTIONS

In the story below, circle all 15 of the adverbs. All the adverbs on this page end with **-ly** and answer the question "how?" about a verb.

THE TALENT SHOW AT THE ZOO

It was the day of the annual talent show at the zoo, and all the animals were busily setting up the equipment. First came the monkeys, who effortlessly swung from trapeze to trapeze. The crowd cheered wildly. Next up were the sea lions, who easily balanced beach balls on their noses. The people cheered enthusiastically. The dolphins swam rapidly around their pool while elegantly flipping themselves out of the water and into the air. The audience clapped loudly. The hippos gracefully performed a ballet in pink tutus, while the kangaroos hopped quickly in and out of rings. The people applauded excitedly. Laughing hyenas told jokes hilariously. Elephants trumpeted their tubas triumphantly. At the end, the parrots, pelicans, puffins, penguins, and pigeons sang bird songs beautifully. Then everyone went home happily, with great memories of a day at the zoo.

The Ultimate Homework Book © 2008 by Marvin Terban, Scholastic Teaching Resources

HOW? WHEN? WHERE?

Many adverbs end with **-ly**. Many other adverbs don't end with **-ly**. Adverbs answer the questions "how?" "where?" and "when?" about a verb. For example:

He ran fast. **How** did he run? Fast.

He ran there. **Where** did he run? There.

He ran today. **When** did he run? Today.

Fast, **there**, and **today** are adverbs because they describe verbs and answer the questions "how?" "where?" and "when?"

DIRECTIONS
Neatly print **how**, **where**, or **when** above each adverb in boldface in the sentences below to show what question it is answering about the verb it is describing.

1. For a 3-year-old, the chimpanzee played the harmonica very **well**.

2. She **never** forgot that amazing game when she hit two home runs.

3. Why was your dog walking **backward** down the hill wearing a dress?

4. My sixth-grade science teacher **always** corrected our tests in green ink.

5. Grandpa worked **hard** for many years looking for gold in the Klondike.

6. Please run **outside** and see if that monster is still sitting in the yard.

7. My aunt **often** put ketchup on her bananas, but only for breakfast.

8. After he broke his ankle in football, he played much **better** than ever.

9. Please put that box of frogs **down** and quietly leave the restaurant.

10. After 106 lessons, my brother dances **worse** than he used to.

The Ultimate Homework Book © © 2008 by Marvin Terban, Scholastic Teaching Resources

ENOUGH WITH VERY ALREADY!

Probably the most overused adverb in the English language is **very**.
For example, people say . . .

- I am very tired.
- The test is very hard.
- My dog is very hairy.
- The music was very loud.
- The soup tastes very salty.
- This computer is very fast.

Very is a perfectly fine word, but it gets boring when you use it all the time. There are many adverbs that mean more or less the same thing as **very**, and if you use them occasionally, your writing will be more interesting and descriptive.

DIRECTIONS
Draw a line through every **very** in the sentences below. Above each one write an adverb from the box. Since there can be more than one adverb to take the place of each **very**, you'll probably be right whichever word you choose.

awfully	enormously	especially	exceptionally
exceedingly	extraordinarily	extremely	immensely
incredibly	particularly	quite	really
remarkably	terribly	tremendously	truly

1. The horror movie we saw was **very** scary, but we're glad we saw it.

2. It's **very** cold out, so wear gloves, a muffler, a hat, and two pairs of socks.

3. Her cousin is **very** tall and bumps his head when he goes through the door.

4. That amazing dessert you created for the bake sale was **very** delicious.

5. I'm **very** grateful for the help you gave me when my goldfish flipped out of its bowl.

6. My sister says she's **very** sorry for breaking your statue of King Kong.

7. The teacher was **very** impressed with my report on pickles in Portugal.

8. The Grand Canyon is a **very** big hole in the ground, don't you think?

9. It was **very** windy that day, and all the beach umbrellas blew away.

10. Freddy was **very** angry when you called him "Freddy frog face."

The Ultimate Homework Book © 2008 by Marvin Terban, Scholastic Teaching Resources

PRESIDENTIAL ANAGRAMS

When you rearrange the letters in a name to create a new word, you make an anagram. For example, if you move around the letters in Columbus, you'll get "Club Sumo," which sounds like a place where huge Japanese wrestlers gather.

DIRECTIONS

In the box below are the names some U.S. of presidents. In the sentences on this page, the letters in their last names have been rearranged to create new words. On the blank line in front of each name in the box, write the number of the sentence whose boldface letters spell that president's last name.

____ John ADAMS	____ Franklin PIERCE
____ James A. GARFIELD	____ Ronald REAGAN
____ William H. HARRISON	____ Theodore ROOSEVELT
____ Rutherford B. HAYES	____ Harry TRUMAN
____ James MADISON	____ Martin VAN BUREN
____ William MCKINLEY	____ George WASHINGTON
____ James MONROE	____ Woodrow WILSON

1. This president did **resolve to** build the Panama Canal.
2. This president **saw nothing** on his way back from crossing the Delaware.
3. Did this president know the **recipe** for English muffins?
4. Many counties, cities, and other **domains** are named after this president.
5. This president put **more on** his plate than he could eat.
6. "Please don't be **sad ma**," said this president to his mother.
7. This president told the courageous church lady that she was a **brave nun**.
8. When asked which instrument he played, this president said, "**A horn, sir**."
9. When asked if he liked his job, this president answered, "**Ah, yes**."
10. After this president gave food to his daughter, she was **a fed girl**.
11. When this president saw the coin on the ground, he shouted, "**My nickel!**"
12. This president wondered what there was **in owls** that made them hoot.
13. This president told his mother, "**Ma, turn** the wheel to the left."
14. This president always liked to ride his horse on **a range**.

The Ultimate Homework Book © 2008 by Marvin Terban, Scholastic Teaching Resources

SINGULAR NOUNS? ADD 'S!

Singular means one person, place, thing, or idea.

Possessive means showing ownership.

If you want to make a singular noun show ownership, just add **'s**. Follow that rule and you will never be wrong. For example:

> My boss**'s** car crashed into Charles**'s** fruit stand and a million blueberries rolled right over the boy**'s** foot onto the lady**'s** new shoes.

DIRECTIONS

In the sentences below, make the nouns in boldface into possessive nouns. All the nouns in boldface in these sentences are singular, so just follow the instructions above.

1. The **girl**   blonde hair blew wildly in the sudden wind.

2. The **dog**   barking scared the goose; soon the **goose**   feathers were flying all over the grass.

3. I polished **Mr. Thomas**   boots until I could see my face in them.

4. The **ox**   tail started swishing rapidly, but the **cow**   tail didn't move.

5. In the restaurant, the **baby**   cries were disturbing **people**   dinners.

6. The men knew a deer was nearby because they saw the **deer**   tracks.

7. If you see **Dennis**   daughter, tell her **Mr. Schwartz**   car is ready.

8. If this is the **girl**   uniform, where are her **sister**   bat and glove?

9. My **class**   science project won the first prize at our **school**   annual fair.

10. I think the cat just stole the **mouse**   piece of cheese.

The Ultimate Homework Book © 2008 by Marvin Terban, Scholastic Teaching Resources

S OR NOT S? LOOK AT THE END!

Plural nouns show more than one person, place, thing, or idea.

Possessive nouns show ownership.

To turn a plural noun into a possessive one, first you have to look at the last letter of that noun and then follow the rules below:

RULES	EXAMPLES
If the last letter of a plural noun is **s**, just add **'** (an apostrophe), and it is possessive.	• The ladies' room is on the third floor. • The two boys' muddy footprints were on the rug. • All the cats' meows made a lot of noise.
If the last letter of a plural noun is **not s**, add **'s**, and it is possessive.	• The men**'s** room is on the fourth floor. • The mice**'s** squeaks woke the children up. • The oxen**'s** tails were neatly braided.

DIRECTIONS

Turn the singular nouns in the first column into plural nouns and write them in the second column. Then show what you would add to make them plural possessive nouns in the third column. Remember to look at the last letter of the plural noun before you add **'** or **'s**. If the last letter is **s**, just add **'**. If the last letter is **not s**, add **'s**.

> The extra words suggest how the plural possessive noun might be used in a phrase.

SINGULAR NOUN	PLURAL NOUN	PLURAL POSSESSIVE NOUN
1. bird		feathers
2. moose		hooves
3. artist		paintbrushes
4. fox		tracks
5. brother		clothes
6. goose		beaks
7. pilot		union
8. child		toys
9. woman		coats
10. sheep		food

The Ultimate Homework Book © 2008 by Marvin Terban, Scholastic Teaching Resources

WHERE DOES THAT APOSTROPHE GO?

Singular means one person, place, thing or idea.

Plural means more than one.

Possessive means showing ownership.

If a noun is singular, always add **'s** to make it possessive. If a noun is plural, look at the last letter. If it's **s**, just add **'** (an apostrophe). If it's **not s**, add **'s**.

DIRECTIONS

Add **'s** to all the singular nouns in boldface in the sentences below to make them possessive. According to the rules, add **'** or **'s** to all the plural nouns to make them possessive. Make sure to look at the last letter of the plural noun before you decide whether to add **'s** or just **'**.

1. The **dragon**　fiery breath burned a hole in the **queen**　castle.

2. The **soldiers**　uniforms were neatly pressed.

3. The **kids**　favorite desserts were always my **mother**　special treats.

4. We watched the **president**　speech on the TV in my **brother**　van.

5. Grandpa kept **Liz**　school picture in his wallet, and showed it to **Harris**　son.

6. Please get the **oxen**　yokes and hitch them to the wagon.

7. The **ladies**　hat department is here; the **men**　shoe department is downstairs.

8. My **cousin**　best job was being a clown at **children**　birthday parties.

9. **Suzy**　**gerbil**　cage needs a good cleaning.

10. **Mrs. Diaz**　car broke down, so she had to borrow her **boss**　car for today.

The Ultimate Homework Book © 2008 by Marvin Terban, Scholastic Teaching Resources

SQUEEZING WORDS TOGETHER

A contraction is a word made by squeezing two words together into one word and leaving out some letters. For example:

can + not = can't   I + will = I'll

TIP
Remember to put an apostrophe where the missing letters used to be.

DIRECTIONS
In the sentences below, join the two words in boldface together into one word and put an apostrophe where the missing letters used to be. Write the contraction on the blank line.

1. **(I am)** _____ so tired, I could lie right down on that pile of rocks and fall asleep.

2. Do you realize that **(we have)** _____ been walking around in circles?

3. **(He has)** _____ given away all his money and moved to Tibet to seek peace and quiet, but all he will find there is yak! yak! yak!

4. I hope she knows that **(she will)** _____ have exactly 12 seconds to climb down the rubber ladder, eat the chocolate-covered lizard, jump into the pool filled with pancake syrup, and find the wooden nose.

5. Ladies and gentleman, **(we are)** _____ very happy to be back in our little hometown after our travels around the universe.

6. I am positive that little Ivan **(will not)** _____ teach the goldfish how to whistle in Russian because he knows that could be annoying.

7. Grandma said to Grandpa, "**(That will)** _____ be all, dear," and she took him home in a wheelbarrow.

8. It was so foggy, the pilot **(could not)** _____ see the airport.

9. **(There has)** _____ been a lot of confusion about Professor Puffenhower's Theory of the Dancing Ducks ever since he first tried to explain it.

10. You absolutely **(must not)** _____ say the word *flugelhorn* to him when he sneezes, or I don't know what he'll do.

The Ultimate Homework Book © 2008 by Marvin Terban, Scholastic Teaching Resources

CONTRACTION REACTION

A contraction is a word made by squeezing two words together into one word and leaving out some letters. For example:

do + not = don't   he + will = he'll

TiP
Remember to put an apostrophe where the missing letters used to be.

DIRECTIONS
In the sentences below, join the two words in boldface together into one word and put an apostrophe where the missing letters used to be. Write the contraction on the blank line.

1. Zippy (**was not**) _____ going to eat his mashed peas, no matter how hungry he was.

2. She told me that (**you have**) _____ got to turn the music down this minute or she's shutting off the electricity in this house.

3. The pig (**has not**) _____ climbed down from the tree since yesterday.

4. Please tell me that my little brother (**did not**) _____ drop his retainer down the drain.

5. I know I (**should not**) _____ eat all the cookies in the bowl, so how about if I leave one for you?

6. (**You would**) _____ be shocked to learn what he did in school today.

7. She told him she (**would not**) _____ marry him even if he were the last man on the planet Mars.

8. When the dentist pulls your tooth, (**it will**) _____ hurt just a bit (maybe).

9. You (**are not**) _____ going to dress up as a baked potato for Halloween, are you?

10. (**I would**) _____ prefer it if you didn't tickle me with that ostrich feather every time I say, "Gadzooks!"

The Ultimate Homework Book © 2008 by Marvin Terban, Scholastic Teaching Resources

WHICH ONE IS THE CONTRACTION?

Sometimes contractions sound like other words that are not contractions. Try not to confuse them. A contraction must be two words put together with an apostrophe taking the place of the missing letter or letters. The other word is just another word.

DIRECTIONS

At the beginning of each sentence below, there are two or more words. Use these words to fill in the blank lines in the sentences. Make sure you put the right word on the right line. One of the words is a contraction, but each can fit into the sentence correctly if you put it in its right place.

1. **(it's, its)** Because _____ such a beautiful day, my dog wants to go outside and play with _____ ball.

2. **(you're, your)** _____ mother says that _____ late for the school bus.

3. **(who's, whose)** We have to let the coach know _____ going in _____ car.

4. **(he'll, heal, heel)** If the bottom of your foot hurts, take your aching _____ to a foot doctor and _____ _____ it.

5. **(he'd, heed)** My grandfather was very strict, and if I didn't _____ his warnings, _____ be angry with me.

6. **(we'd, weed)** Today _____ better _____ the garden before it rains.

7. **(let's, lets)** If the teacher _____ us, _____ leave early for band rehearsal.

8. **(we'll, wheel)** _____ be able to pull the wagon once we get the front _____ fixed.

9. **(they're, their, there)** Where are they? _____ over _____ in _____ tent.

10. **(I'll, isle, aisle)** We will be married on the island, and then _____ walk you down the _____ on the _____ .

The Ultimate Homework Book © 2008 by Marvin Terban, Scholastic Teaching Resources

MAKE IT BIG!

Capital letters are very important. Here are four places to use capital letters when you write:

1. Capitalize the first word in a sentence.

    Don't forget to bring the frogs to school on Thursday.

2. Capitalize the pronoun I.

    Will I will ever be as tall as my father?

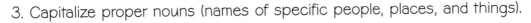

3. Capitalize proper nouns (names of specific people, places, and things).

    George Washington Carver was famous for what he did
    with peanuts.

4. Capitalize proper adjectives.

    I ate an American steak with Italian olives and French bread.

DIRECTIONS

Imagine that your computer keyboard has broken and you can't type any capital letters. You have to finish the sentences below for homework. Put a line through any lowercase letter in the sentences below that should be capitalized and print the capital letter above it.

1. "idaho potatoes go well with maine lobsters," says audrey, the cook.

2. at the museum of european art, there's an exhibit of dutch paintings.

3. thomas edison failed many times before he invented the lightbulb.

4. if i told him once, i told him a thousand times that i don't tap dance.

5. do you want chinese egg rolls, japanese sushi, or mexican quesadillas?

6. the first american film star, charlie chaplin, was born in london.

7. the lady from spain was amazed when i spoke to her in perfect spanish.

8. things from thailand are thai; things from switzerland are swiss.

The Ultimate Homework Book © 2008 by Marvin Terban, Scholastic Teaching Resources

CAPITAL IDEA!

Capital letters are extremely important. Here are four places to use capital letters when you write.

1. Capitalize abbreviations of titles after someone's name.

    Martin Luther King, Jr., was the youngest winner of the Nobel Peace Prize.

2. Capitalize the titles of family members when they are used with their names.

    I saw Aunt Loraine and Uncle George at the mall.

3. Capitalize the titles of family members if you are speaking or writing directly to them, even if you don't use their names.

    Thanks for the beautiful gift, Grandma.

4. Capitalize titles of specific family members if you are speaking about them without using their names. (It's as if their titles are their names.)

    Grandpa, did you tell Mom that you gave Dad a new fishing rod?

DIRECTIONS

Imagine that the sign maker forgot to load any capital letters onto his truck. You're his assistant and you have to help him deliver the words below. Put a line through any lowercase letter in the sentences below that should be capitalized and neatly print the capital letter above it.

1. grandmother freedman baked cousin laurie a pink wedding cake.

2. tomorrow, mother, i'll meet richard farnsworth, esq., at the palace.

3. is grandma shirley uncle lewis's mother or his sister?

4. dad, did you know dr. timothy james williams on long island?

5. that's aunt bonnie and kurt westerman, sr., in iceland last year.

6. please, grandfather, don't ride your motorcycle through the petunias.

7. mom, dad, my report card really isn't as bad as you'll think it is.

8. franklin roosevelt, jr., had the same name as his father, the president.

The Ultimate Homework Book © 2008 by Marvin Terban, Scholastic Teaching Resources

THE BIGGER, THE BETTER

Capital letters are extremely important. Here are four places to use capital letters when you write.

1. Capitalize school subjects when they are the names of languages.

   French, Latin, Spanish (but not math, science, or history)

2. Capitalize the first, last, and all important words in the names of school subjects when they are specific courses listed in a school or college catalog.

   Introduction to Issues of Global Environment

3. Capitalize geographic locations when they refer to specific places on the map or sections of a country, not just directions.

   There's more open land in the West and more crowded cities in the East.

4. Capitalize the names of holidays, festivals, and special events.

   Christmas, Rosh Hashanah, Id al-Fitr, Kwanzaa, Columbus Day

DIRECTIONS

Imagine a giant bookworm has been slithering through books and devouring all the capital letters. Now you must counteract his voracious appetite and put the eaten letters back. Put a line through any lowercase letter in the sentences below that should be capitalized and neatly print the capital letter above it.

1. at the school for brilliant babies i learned chinese in kindergarten.

2. my mother came from the northwest, my father from the southeast.

3. my favorite class at kilmer college was called laughable literature.

4. people wear big hats and parade in the streets on easter sunday.

5. they were studying arabic and amharic at the african folk festival.

6. you have to learn swedish to take the sweden swings course.

7. yom kippur and good friday are very special holidays.

8. curiously, the annual winter wonderland fair is held every other year.

The Ultimate Homework Book © 2008 by Marvin Terban, Scholastic Teaching Resources

STAND UP TALL!

Capital letters are extremely important. Here are four places to use capital letters when you write.

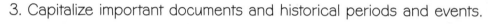

1. Capitalize deities (gods and goddesses), key religious figures, and holy books and documents.

    Allah, Buddha, Vishnu, Bible, Talmud

2. Capitalize the names of all the planets in the solar system, including Earth (but not sun and moon).

    Mars, Jupiter, Neptune

3. Capitalize important documents and historical periods and events.

    Magna Carta, Middle Ages, Renaissance, Revolutionary War

4. Capitalize the brand names of products.

    Kellogg's, Panasonic, Tide

DIRECTIONS

A strange shrinking illness has overtaken all capital letters in the land. Because they're bigger than other letters, they've become too weak to stand up to their full uppercase height. It's your job to make them upright again. Put a line through any lowercase letter in the sentences below that should be capitalized and neatly print the capital letter above it.

1. the rings of saturn make it one of the most beautiful planets.

2. franklin signed the declaration of independence and the constitution.

3. please get me some cheerios, kleenex, and scotch tape at the store.

4. my grandparents lived during the depression and korean war.

5. i put goodyear tires on my general motors car.

6. genesis, ecclesiastes, exodus, and leviticus are books of the bible.

7. we studied the boston tea party and the battle of bunker hill in history.

8. venus is way too hot. i'll stay here on earth, thank you.

The Ultimate Homework Book © 2008 by Marvin Terban, Scholastic Teaching Resources

BIG AND PROUD!

Capital letters are extremely important. Here are four places to use capital letters when you write.

1. Capitalize the names of languages.

   Spanish, English, Swahili, Chinese

2. Capitalize religions, tribes, ethnic groups, and nationalities.

   Apache, Buddhist, Christian, Irish American, Islam, Israeli, Muslim

3. Capitalize names of companies, stores, and businesses.

   Apple Computer, Inc., Sharper Image

4. Capitalize the first word in a direct quotation.

   The teacher said, "There's no homework tonight!"

DIRECTIONS

Imagine a tornado has swept through the library and blown away all the capital letters in all the books. You have to rescue the books from lowercase-itis. Put a line through any lowercase letter in the sentences below that should be capitalized and print the capital letter above it.

1. the translator at the united nations speaks swahili, tsonga, and zulu.

2. they're building a new starbucks next to radio shack.

3. did you say, "peanut butter is stuck on my nose"?

4. which is harder to learn: japanese, chinese, or vietnamese?

5. are they having a clearance sale at gap or macy's?

6. do you like the burgers at mcdonald's, wendy's, or burger king best?

7. some italian americans speak both italian and english.

8. my grandpa always says to me, "you're the apple of my eye."

9. christians, muslims, hindus, buddhists, and jews all live in this city.

10. lincoln once declared, "fourscore and seven years ago . . . ."

The Ultimate Homework Book © 2008 by Marvin Terban, Scholastic Teaching Resources

STANDING TALL!

Capital letters are extremely important. Here are three places to use capital letters when you write.

1. Capitalize official titles or positions when they come in front of a person's name.

    General William T. Sherman fought in the Civil War.

2. Capitalize days of the week.

    Monday, Tuesday, Wednesday, etc.

3. Capitalize the first, last, and all the main words in the title of a book, movie, song, play, musical show, opera, magazine, newspaper, television show, or radio program. (Note: The song title below is in quotes. All other titles are in italics.)

    Last week I read **H**arry **P**otter and the **H**alf-**B**lood **P**rince.

Do not capitalize a short word (like **the, a, an, of, in, by,** or **for**) unless it is the first or last word in a title: *The Phantom Tollbooth*

DIRECTIONS

While the alphabet was making a sea voyage, the capital letters were washed away by a giant wave. The sentences below must arrive at their destination with capital letters. Save the day. Put a line through any lowercase letter that should be capitalized and neatly print the capital letter above it.

1. mrs. consuela schlepkis is a good friend of miss karen youngman.

2. in my opinion, *gone with the wind* is the greatest movie ever made.

3. i told you my canary's birthday was thursday, not sunday!

4. my teacher assigned us 10 pages to read in *the history of the world.*

5. dr. christiaan barnard performed the first human heart transplant.

6. i got singing roles in both *the sound of music* and *the wizard of oz.*

7. capt. edward is being interviewed on the radio show *heroic heroes.*

8. prof. piano sang "the star-spangled banner" at the ball game on monday.

9. on saturdays mr. w. t. james reads *the daily bugle* for an hour.

10. i missed the last episode of *a lovely life* on television last monday.

The Ultimate Homework Book © 2008 by Marvin Terban, Scholastic Teaching Resources

CAP IT UP!

Capital letters are very important. Here are four places to use capital letters when you write.

1. Capitalize months of the year.

    January, February, March, etc.

    Do not capitalize the names of the seasons: summer, fall, winter, spring.

2. Capitalize the first word in the greeting (salutation) of a friendly letter.

    Dear Roslyn,   Hello, Cindy,

3. Capitalize the first word and all the main words in the greeting (salutation) of a business letter.

    To Whom It May Concern:

4. Capitalize the first word in the closing of any letter, friendly or business.

    Warmest wishes,   Sincerely yours,

DIRECTIONS

The King of Lower Kaysovia has banned all capital letters. You must defy the king and put the capitals back into letters that the people of the kingdom send each other so they can read them. Put a line through any lowercase letter that should be capitalized and neatly print the capital letter above it.

dear party decoration committee:

i don't think it would be a good idea to decorate our halloween party in october with purple pumpkins. pumpkins are definitely orange.

thank you for your consideration.

yours truly,
henry j. artsy

dear customer service department:

i bought a pair of your zippy brand sneakers in august. i washed them just once in september, and they shrank so much that now only my little cat can fit in them. how can i stretch them?

gratefully yours,
miss isla ubiles

The Ultimate Homework Book © 2008 by Marvin Terban, Scholastic Teaching Resources

GETTING IT TOGETHER

Compound words are made by putting two or more words together. For example:

When you get **home** from school, you have **work** to do.

Home + **work** = homework. **Homework** is a compound word.

DIRECTIONS

From the 20 words below, choose two for each line to put together to make a compound word. Write each completed compound in the last column. There are clues to help you make 10 compound words.

blood	book	boy	brush	cow	cut	fish
flash	gold	grass	hair	hopper	hound
light	note	snow	storm	tooth	watch	wrist

CLUE	FIRST WORD	+	SECOND WORD	=	COMPOUND WORD
1. What a barber gives you		+		=	
2. A jumping insect		+		=	
3. What you hold in your hand to see in the dark		+		=	
4. Dog with a great sense of smell		+		=	
5. Cattleman on horseback		+		=	
6. Small, orange-yellow carp		+		=	
7. Bound blank writing pages		+		=	
8. Small tool to clean what you bite with		+		=	
9. Timepiece worn above hand		+		=	
10. A blizzard		+		=	

The Ultimate Homework Book © 2008 by Marvin Terban, Scholastic Teaching Resources

1 WORD + 1 WORD = 1 WORD

Compound words are made by putting two or more words together. For example:

You pack a **suit** into a **case**.

Suit + case = suitcase. Suitcase is a compound word.

DIRECTIONS

From the 20 words below, choose two for each line to put together to make a compound word. Write each completed compound in the last column. There are clues to help you make 10 compound words.

ball	basket	board	boat	class	clip	cloth
cycle	fire	flower	gentle	house	land	
lord	man	mate	motor	pot	row	wash

CLUE	FIRST WORD	+	SECOND WORD	=	COMPOUND WORD
1. Sphere used to shoot hoops		+		=	
2. Fellow student		+		=	
3. Building where red engines are		+		=	
4. Small, paddled water vehicle		+		=	
5. A person who rents apartments		+		=	
6. Container for plants		+		=	
7. Flat, portable paper-holder		+		=	
8. Two-wheeled road vehicle		+		=	
9. A cultured, polite male		+		=	
10. Piece of material to clean the body		+		=	

The Ultimate Homework Book © 2008 by Marvin Terban, Scholastic Teaching Resources

ONE WORD FROM TWO

Compound words are made by putting two or more words together. For example:

Sometimes rain will **pour down** from the sky.

Down + pour = downpour. Downpour is a compound word.

DIRECTIONS

From the 20 words below, choose two for each line to put together to make a compound word. Write each completed compound in the last column. There are clues to help you make 10 compound words.

basket	beam	black	board	cake	camp	cup
	dog	drug	earth	fire	paper	quake	
rattle	sand	snake	store	sun	waste	watch

CLUE	FIRST WORD	+	SECOND WORD	=	COMPOUND WORD
1. What the teacher writes on with chalk		+		=	
2. A violent shaking of the ground		+		=	
3. Ray of light from solar system star		+		=	
4. Place to get prescriptions filled		+		=	
5. Trash container		+		=	
6. Canine that guards your property		+		=	
7. Outdoor burning logs (to roast marshmallows)		+		=	
8. Rough sheet you use to smooth wood		+		=	
9. Poisonous, limbless reptile with noisy tail		+		=	
10. Small pastry baked in paper mold		+		=	

The Ultimate Homework Book © 2008 by Marvin Terban, Scholastic Teaching Resources

A MARRIAGE OF WORDS

Compound words are made by putting two or more words together. For example:

News is printed on **paper**.

News + **paper** = newspaper. **Newspaper** is a compound word.

DIRECTIONS

From the 20 words below, choose two for each line to put together to make a compound word. Write each completed compound in the last column. There are clues to help you make 10 compound words.

ball	bean	bow	chair	corn	dragon	eye
field	fly	guard	high	jelly	life	
out	pass	pig	pop	rain	tail	word

CLUE	FIRST WORD	+	SECOND WORD	=	COMPOUND WORD
1. Insect with four transparent wings		+		=	
2. Tall chair for babies at mealtimes		+		=	
3. Hard candy with fruit center		+		=	
4. What you see with		+		=	
5. Rescuer of drowning swimmers		+		=	
6. Grassy area beyond the diamond		+		=	
7. Braided hair at back of the head		+		=	
8. Color arc in the sky after a shower		+		=	
9. Kernels heated until they explode		+		=	
10. Lets you into computer program		+		=	

The Ultimate Homework Book © 2008 by Marvin Terban, Scholastic Teaching Resources

WORDWORDS

Compound words are made by putting two or more words together. For example:

A trained person on a beach or by a pool works to **guard** your **life**.

Life + guard = lifeguard. Lifeguard is a compound word.

DIRECTIONS

From the 20 words below, choose two for each line to put together to make a compound word. Write each completed compound in the last column. There are clues to help you make 10 compound words.

ache	bar	bath	coat	cross	fall	flag
	handle	head	lace	over	pole	rail
road	room	ship	shoe	walk	water	wreck

CLUE	FIRST WORD	+	SECOND WORD	=	COMPOUND WORD
1. Upright shaft from which a banner flies		+		=	
2. Heavy, long outer garment		+		=	
3. Steel tracks that a train rides on		+		=	
4. A marked place on a street to walk safely		+		=	
5. What you grip to steer a bicycle		+		=	
6. Cascade where river goes over the edge		+		=	
7. A pain in your skull		+		=	
8. The cord that keeps your footwear tied		+		=	
9. Place to take shower, wash hands, etc.		+		=	
10. The sinking and destruction of a vessel at sea		+		=	

The Ultimate Homework Book © 2008 by Marvin Terban, Scholastic Teaching Resources

GLUE WORDS

Conjunctions are words that join words or parts of sentences together. The three most common conjunctions are **and**, **or**, and **but**. Each one means something different.

> **And** joins words or phrases that go together equally.
>
> **Or** gives you a choice.
>
> **But** introduces something that contrasts with something earlier in the sentence.

DIRECTIONS

Write **and**, **or**, or **but** on the blank lines where you think they belong.

1. I completely forgot to study for the big math test, _____ amazingly, I still got all the answers right.

2. He saved his money for a whole year, _____ he bought himself a new bicycle.

3. "Either clean up this room this minute," her mother said, "_____ you're not going to the movies tonight!"

4. The weather was beautiful, _____ everyone loved the parade.

5. Would you like Italian _____ Chinese food for dinner?

6. Her face was dirty, her clothes were torn, and she was far from the palace, _____ I immediately knew she was the princess.

7. He was selected "Student of the Year" because he got the highest grades, was elected class president, _____ raised the most money in the charity marathon.

8. I don't have much money left, so I can buy either a pizza _____ my favorite magazine, but not both.

9. I memorized the whole script before the auditions and acted my heart and soul out for the director, _____ I still didn't get a part in the play.

10. I can't decide which dog to adopt from the animal rescue league: the pretty Pomeranian _____ the dashing Dalmatian.

The Ultimate Homework Book © 2008 by Marvin Terban, Scholastic Teaching Resources

DRESSY WORDS

An eponym is the name of a person or place that has become a real word in English. For example, today we measure temperature in degrees Fahrenheit. Water freezes at 32° Fahrenheit. But did you know that Gabriel Fahrenheit was a German physicist in the 1700s who invented the scale that we use to measure temperature? Mr. Fahrenheit's name is an eponym.

DIRECTIONS

Below are the names of five people and one place. These names have become common English words that name articles of clothing. On the blank lines above each name, write the number of the paragraph that you think describes that person or place.

_____	_____	_____
Amelia J. Bloomer	Bikini Atoll	Jules Léotard
_____	_____	_____
Levi Strauss	Lord Cardigan	Pantaloon

1. In the 1400s in Italy, people laughed at a funny character in popular comedy shows. No matter who played his part, the actor always wore the same kind of trousers, and today the first syllable of this character's name means "trousers."

2. A famous circus performer in France in the mid-1800s designed his own stretchy, tight costume to wear when performing his aerial somersaults. The costume took his name, and today dancers, acrobats, and gymnasts wear it.

3. She was the editor of an American magazine for women in the 1800s. She fought for women's rights, including the right to wear comfortable clothing. Her last name became the name of the two-piece sports outfit she designed to be worn under a short skirt.

4. In the mid-1800s in England there lived a strict general of the British army. He often wore an open, woolen sweater without a collar to keep warm. This general was so famous that his name became the name of the sweater.

5. This man's first name became the name of the heavy blue overalls he manufactured for the people who rushed to California in the mid-1800s to mine for gold. These pants are still popular today.

6. The United States began testing atom bombs in 1946 on a little island in the Pacific Ocean. That summer, people at a Paris fashion show saw a new skimpy, two-piece ladies' bathing suit for the first time. Some people joked that the bathing suits "hit the audience like an atom bomb." So the name of the island where the bombs were tested became the name of the bathing suit.

The Ultimate Homework Book © 2008 by Marvin Terban, Scholastic Teaching Resources

EDIBLE WORDS

An eponym is the name of a person or place that has become a real word in English. For example, a general in the American Civil War wore big whiskers down the sides of his face. His name was Ambrose Burnside. Other men copied him, and today we call this facial hair "sideburns."

DIRECTIONS
Below are the names of two people and four places. These names have become common English words that name articles of food. On the blank lines above each name, write the number of the paragraph that you think describes that person or place.

_____	_____	_____
Bologna, Italy	Cheddar, England	Earl of Sandwich
_____	_____	_____
Frankfurt, Germany	Hamburg, Germany	Sylvester Graham

1. The meat patties that were first made in this European city made the city famous. Today they're eaten on buns and enjoyed at barbeques and fast food restaurants.

2. This man thought meats, white bread, and alcoholic beverages were unhealthy for people. So in the 1800s he baked up his own healthful cracker, and it became very popular. The cracker is still made today, and it's named after him.

3. A long time ago in a little village, a cheese maker created this hard, smooth cheese. It comes in yellow or white, and it can be mild or sharp in flavor. The name of the village is the name of the cheese.

4. In this picturesque city, people loved eating seasoned smoked sausages made of mixed meats. Soon people all over the world were eating them or slicing them into sandwiches. Today the city's name is the sausage's name.

5. This British nobleman loved to play cards all night. When he got hungry, he'd eat a piece of meat with his bare hands. But that made the cards greasy, so he put the meat between two pieces of bread to keep his hands clean. That's how he invented the kind of meal that bears his name today.

6. The nickname we use today for these delicious sausages sounds like an overheated canine, but they made the European city where they originated famous. What would a baseball game be today without one of them smothered in ketchup, mustard, onions, or sauerkraut?

The Ultimate Homework Book © 2008 by Marvin Terban, Scholastic Teaching Resources

THING WORDS

An eponym is the name of a person or place that has become a real word in English. For example, the long and short beeps or flashes of light that we call Morse code were devised by Samuel F. B. Morse, in the 1800s. The code is named after him.

DIRECTIONS
Below are the names of six people whose names have become common English words. On the blank lines above each name, write the number of the paragraph that you think describes that person.

＿＿＿＿＿	＿＿＿＿＿	＿＿＿＿＿
George W. Ferris	Joseph Guillotin	Louis Braille
＿＿＿＿＿	＿＿＿＿＿	＿＿＿＿＿
Robert Bunsen	Theodore Roosevelt	Antoine J. Sax

1. In science class you might see your teacher doing experiments using a small metal tube on a stand that burns gas and air. This device is named after the German chemist who invented it in 1855 for his own experiments.

2. By the time he was 15 years old in the early 1800s, this blind French boy had developed a way for blind people to read books by touching raised dots on a page. This system of writing and printing was named after him.

3. During the French Revolution in the late 1700s, a doctor urged the government to get a beheading machine he'd heard about. When it was named after him, the members of his family were so ashamed they changed their name!

4. If you've ever heard a jazz band play, you've heard the sounds of a metal wind instrument invented by and named after an instrument maker from Belgium. He played it in public for the first time in Paris in 1844.

5. At the 1893 Chicago World's Fair, people flocked to ride on a huge revolving wheel that carried almost 1,500 people up and around. It was designed by an American engineer. The spectacular ride is popular at amusement parks around the world. It's named after its inventor.

6. The 26th president of the U.S. liked to go hunting. In 1902, as the famous story goes, someone tied a bear to a tree so that the president could shoot it without trouble. He refused. Ever since, toy companies have produced stuffed bears named for this president's nickname.

The Ultimate Homework Book © 2008 by Marvin Terban, Scholastic Teaching Resources

MIXED-UP ANIMALS

Animal experts have been experimenting with crossbreeding animals for many years. These animals are called hybrids. You may already know that a mule has a donkey for a father and a horse for a mother. But do you know these other hybrids?

Father	Mother	Hybrid's Name
camel	llama	CAMA
horse	donkey	HINNY
lion	tiger	LIGER

DIRECTIONS

Imagine you are an animal crossbreeder, but you work with words, not animals. Each word in the box below is the imaginary offspring of a pair of real animals. Match each word to its "parents." For example, a cat and a snake might be parents of a "cake"!

caramel	chickpea	loafer	manager	mobster
monster	scale	tycoon	waiter	weaver

PARENTS	IMAGINARY HYBRIDS
1. llama and gopher	
2. mouse and lobster	
3. walrus and alligator	
4. caribou and camel	
5. wolf and beaver	
6. tiger and raccoon	
7. skunk and whale	
8. manatee and gerbil	
9. monkey and hamster	
10. chicken and peacock	

The Ultimate Homework Book © 2008 by Marvin Terban, Scholastic Teaching Resources

MAKE A NEW ANIMAL

Animal experts have been experimenting with crossbreeding animals for many years. These animals are called hybrids. You may already know that a mule has a donkey for a father and a horse for a mother. But do you know these other hybrids?

Father	Mother	Hybrid's Name
tiger	lion	TIGON
killer whale	dolphin	WOLPHIN
zebra	horse	ZORSE

DIRECTIONS

Imagine you are an animal crossbreeder, but you work with words, not animals. Each word in the box below is the imaginary child of a pair of real animals. Match each word to its "parents." For example, a parakeet and ants might be parents of a "pair of pants."

battle   balloon   cantaloupe   crayon   muffin
musketeer   mustard   pants   toenail   truck

PARENTS	IMAGINARY HYBRIDS
1. mole and puffin	
2. muskrat and lizard	
3. bat and cattle	
4. pig and ants	
5. toad and snail	
6. baboon and loon	
7. muskrat and deer	
8. cat and antelope	
9. trout and buck	
10. crayfish and lion	

The Ultimate Homework Book © 2008 by Marvin Terban, Scholastic Teaching Resources

BONJOUR, FIFI!

Animals make all sorts of sounds. They bark and meow and oink and bray. Those words are in English. In other countries, the sounds that animals make are in that country's language. For example, in America a duck says "quack quack," but in Turkey it says "vach vach."

DIRECTIONS
Look at the unfamiliar words below. Try to imagine what language they're in and what animal would say them. Then, fill in the chart. Since you probably don't talk to animals in other countries a lot, your answers will be your best guesses.

> cleek cleek   cree cree   eee haw   goo goo   hru hru
>
> jip jip   kee-kee-ree-kee   klook klook   kra kra   maaaaa maaaaa
>
> nyan nyan   twee twee   um-moo   wah wah   zzzzz

ANIMAL	HOW IT SOUNDS IN ENGLISH	HOW IT SOUNDS IN A DIFFERENT LANGUAGE
bee	bzzzz bzzzz	Polish:
bird	chirp chirp	Thai:
cat	meow meow	Japanese:
chicken	cluck cluck	Danish:
cow	moo moo	Korean:
cricket	chirp chirp	Italian:
crow	caw caw	Greek:
dog	bow wow	French:
horse	naaaay naaaay	Farsi:
lamb	baaaaa baaaa	German:
monkey	chee chee	Swedish:
mouse	squeak squeak	Hebrew:
pig	oink oink	Russian:
rooster	cock-a-doodle-doo	Spanish:
turkey	gobble gobble	Chinese:

The Ultimate Homework Book © 2008 by Marvin Terban, Scholastic Teaching Resources

BOO-BOO WORDS

For many years, speakers and writers have been making up fun words by taking a word and doubling the sound. For example, someone once wanted to name a new chocolate candy with fruit and nuts in it. He or she took **bon**, which means "good" in French, and doubled it to make **bonbon**. That made it doubly good.

DIRECTIONS
Below is a list of double words. Read each definition and try to figure out which word from the list goes with it. Write it on the blank line. Check with a dictionary to see if you got it right.

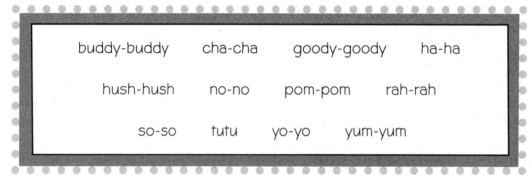

buddy-buddy   cha-cha   goody-goody   ha-ha

hush-hush   no-no   pom-pom   rah-rah

so-so   tutu   yo-yo   yum-yum

1. A person who's too good to be true. _____

2. A Latin American dance with lots of rhythm. _____

3. The sound of laughter. _____

4. Something's that quiet, secret, or confidential. _____

5. Something that you should definitely not do. _____

6. Fluffy paper ball on a stick that cheerleaders wave. _____

7. Something that's not too good and not too bad. _____

8. A short ballet skirt _____

9. A flat spool that you make go up and down on a string. _____

10. This means "This food is delicious." _____

11. Describes people who are full of spirit and enthusiasm. _____

12. Being really, really good friends with someone. _____

The Ultimate Homework Book © 2008 by Marvin Terban, Scholastic Teaching Resources

FIDDLE-FADDLE WORDS

For many years, speakers and writers have been making up fun words by taking words and adding sounds that almost rhyme. For example, someone once took **fiddle**, added **faddle**, and created a new word, **fiddle-faddle**, which means "utter nonsense."

DIRECTIONS

Below is a list of words with their second halves missing. Read the definition for each word and try to figure out what the second half should be. It will almost rhyme with the first half. Write it on the blank line. Check with a dictionary to see if you got it right.

1. Small talk, unimportant conversation: chit _____

2. Train sound: clickety-_____

3. Sound of a horse's hooves: clippety-_____

4. Waste time doing nothing: dilly-_____

5. Sound of a bell ringing: ding _____

6. A trivial gadget or trinket: doo _____

7. Donkey sound: hee-_____

8. Sound of rabbit running: hippety-_____

9. An expression of boredom: ho-_____

10. Everything's just fine: hunky-_____

11. Nonsense word: jibber-_____

12. The sound of metal pieces touching: jingle-_____

13. Small, worthless object or ornament: knick _____

14. Quick light taps or steps: pitter-_____

15. Undesirable people with bad reputations: riff _____

16. Balanced board that goes up and down: see _____

17. Sound of water hitting a surface: splish-_____

18. Sound a clock makes: tick _____

19. Everything's upside down: topsy-_____

20. Turning sharply left and right: zig _____

The Ultimate Homework Book © 2008 by Marvin Terban, Scholastic Teaching Resources

FUDDY-DUDDY WORDS

For many years, speakers and writers have made up fun words by taking words and adding sounds that rhyme. For example, someone wanted to describe a person who was fussy. He or she took the word **dud**, expanded it to **duddy** and rhymed it with **fuddy**, to make **fuddy-duddy**.

DIRECTIONS

Below is a list of words with their second halves missing. Read the definition for each word and try to figure out what the second half should be. It will rhyme with the first half. Write it on the blank line. Check with a dictionary to see if you got it right.

1. A very important person: big _____

2. The sound of crying: boo _____

3. Dog bark: bow _____

4. Everything's fair and equal: even-_____

5. Totally worthless language: clap _____

6. Very, very soft: fuzzy-_____

7. Extremely clever with your hands: handy-_____

8. A nervous and jumpy feeling: heebie-_____

9. Everything is confused and careless: helter-_____

10. Magic tricks and magic words: hocus-_____

11. A confused, messed-up mixture of stuff: hodge _____

12. The common, ordinary people: hoi _____

13. Snobby and snooty: hoity-_____

14. Wow! What a surprise! holy _____

15. A situation that's busy, noisy, and disorganized: hub _____

16. Something that's monotonous and boring: hum _____

17. Extremely tiny: itsy-_____ or teeny-_____

18. The essence of the matter: nitty-_____

19. An ice cream with mixed fruits: tutti-_____

20. Very huggy-kissy and affectionate: lovey-_____

The Ultimate Homework Book © 2008 by Marvin Terban, Scholastic Teaching Resources

BE AN ANIMAL DETECTIVE

If you ever tried to find a cat that didn't want to be found, you know that animals can hide themselves in very clever places so as not to be discovered. They can even hide in words! For example, there is a "cat" hiding in **catch**.

DIRECTIONS

An animal is hiding in each of the words below. In one word, two animals are hiding. Be an animal detective and find the animals hidden in these words.

TiPS
- There are three "cats" hiding on the list.
- One word has two animals hiding in it!

HIDING WORDS	HIDDEN ANIMALS
1. acrobat	_____
2. antique	_____
3. beard	_____
4. beef	_____
5. board	_____
6. boondoggle	_____
7. bullion	_____
8. catastrophe	_____
9. coward	_____
10. crowbar	_____
11. delicatessen	_____
12. escape	_____
13. fowl	_____
14. goatee	_____
15. magnum	_____
16. pigment	_____
17. pumice	_____
18. scatter	_____
19. scrabble	_____
20. scratch	_____
21. selfish	_____
22. spigot	_____
23. wheel	_____

The Ultimate Homework Book © 2008 by Marvin Terban, Scholastic Teaching Resources

SIMPLE SAYINGS, BIG WORDS

Having a big vocabulary is terrific, but sometimes you can overdo it.

DIRECTIONS

Below are five famous sayings and what they mean. Below that are the same sayings rewritten with big vocabulary. Use a good dictionary and your smart brain to figure out how to match the famous sayings to their big-vocabulary versions. On the blank lines in front of the big-vocabulary versions, put the number of the famous saying in its original version.

a. A fool and his money are soon parted.
People who aren't careful about their money will quickly lose it.

b. A rolling stone gathers no moss.
People who keep moving around and don't settle down in one place have no roots (home, friends, job, etc.) or responsibilities.

c. All that glitters is not gold.
Something may look good at first, but watch out! It could be worthless.

d. People who live in glass houses shouldn't throw stones.
Nobody's perfect, so don't criticize other people's faults because you have faults of your own that others can see.

e. Too many cooks spoil the broth.
If too many people with different opinions work together on a single project, it will get messed up.

1. _____ A solid, nonmetallic, earthy material rotating on its axis will not accumulate an accretion of bryophytic plant growth.

2. _____ A superfluousness of persons skilled in the preparation of gastronomic creations will impair the quality of a liquid stock in which meat, fish, or vegetables are cooked.

3. _____ Everything that sparkles with effulgence is not a yellow, malleable, ductile metallic element that is aurous.

4. _____ An imprudent blockhead and his currency will rapidly disassociate from each another.

5. _____ Residents who inhabit domiciles constructed of a hard, brittle, transparent substance should refrain from projecting small bits of solid mineral material.

The Ultimate Homework Book © 2008 by Marvin Terban, Scholastic Teaching Resources

WHAT DID YOU SAY?

Having a big vocabulary is terrific, but sometimes you can overdo it.

DIRECTIONS
Below are five famous sayings and what they mean. Below that are the same sayings rewritten with big vocabulary. Use a good dictionary and your smart brain to figure out how to match the famous sayings to their big-vocabulary versions. On the blank lines in front of the big-vocabulary versions, put the number of the famous saying in its original version.

---

a. The early bird catches the worm.
If you want to accomplish something, don't delay. Get up and do it!

b. You can lead a horse to water, but you can't make it drink.
You can offer a person a good opportunity or smart advice, but you can't force that person to do what you think is best.

c. Money is the root of all evil
A lot of bad things in life are caused by people's desire for riches.

d. Waste not, want not.
If you don't waste anything (like money, food, your health, etc.) you'll have it when you need it.

e. Don't count your chickens before they hatch.
Don't be so sure that something good will happen to you until it really does.

---

1. _____ Do not expend prodigally, and you will not lack needfully.

2. _____ Currency is the fundamental essence of everything that is malevolent.

3. _____ It is within your ability to usher an equine quadruped to a compound of oxygen and hydrogen; however, you will be unable to coerce the beast to imbibe the liquid.

4. _____ The non-procrastinating, warm-blooded, egg-laying, feathered, flying vertebrate ensnares the burrowing, soft-bodied, limbless invertebrate.

5. _____ Do not determine the total number of domestic fowl you have prior to their emerging from their eggs.

The Ultimate Homework Book © 2008 by Marvin Terban, Scholastic Teaching Resources

HUH? WHAT WAS THAT AGAIN?

Having a big vocabulary is terrific, but sometimes you can overdo it.

DIRECTIONS

Below are five famous sayings and what they mean. Below that are the same sayings rewritten with big vocabulary. Use a good dictionary and your smart brain to figure out how to match the famous sayings to their big-vocabulary versions. On the blank lines in front of the big-vocabulary versions, put the number of the famous saying in its original version.

a. An apple a day keeps the doctor away.
Living a healthful lifestyle (like eating fruits and vegetables instead of junk food) will keep you from getting sick.

b. To err is human, to forgive divine.
Anybody can make a mistake. That's acting normal. When you forgive someone who's made a mistake, that's acting like a god.

c. Don't lock the barn door after the horse is stolen.
When you know there's a possibility that something bad can happen, take action in advance to prevent it from happening.

d. Make hay while the sun shines.
Take advantage of good opportunities when they're available. Get your jobs done when conditions are favorable.

e. Look before you leap.
Don't act hastily. Before you do anything, especially something risky, stop and think about all the consequences of your actions.

1. ____ Exercise circumspection prior to propelling yourself precariously.

2. ____ Blundering is characteristic of Homo sapiens; exoneration is characteristic of a celestial being.

3. ____ Do not secure the fastener on the portal to the stable subsequent to the larceny of the equine.

4. ____ A quotidian round red fruit of the rose family impedes the necessity for medical care.

5. ____ Mow and dry the grass during the time that the central body in the solar system is emitting illumination.

The Ultimate Homework Book © 2008 by Marvin Terban, Scholastic Teaching Resources

SPELL-ALIKE WORDS

Homographs are words that are spelled the same but often sound different. For example:

- The word **dove** could be either a bird (**dove** rhymes with **love**) or the past tense of the verb to **dive** (**dove** rhymes with **stove**).

- **Use** can be pronounced with an **s** or a **z** sound: I make good **use** of my brain when I **use** it.

- Sometimes the accent falls on the first syllable, sometimes on the second: If his **con**duct improves, he will con**duct** the school orchestra.

- Sometimes one of the homographs is capitalized and the other one isn't.

DIRECTIONS

Complete each sentence by choosing a word from the box below and writing a pair of homographs on the blank lines. When you read the sentence aloud, pronounce the two words differently. The sentence will still make sense. There are clues in parentheses to help you figure out the missing homographs.

produce   buffet   read   desert   excuse   rebel   suspect   does

1. _____ (rhymes with fuzz) she like male deer or _____ (female deer)?

2. "_____ (pardon) me," said the principal, "I do not accept your _____ (reason) for being late to school."

3. "He is my primary _____ (a person thought to have committed a crime)," said the detective, "because I _____ (believe) him of doing the crime."

4. Did the hurricane winds _____ (knock against) the party guests and knock over the _____ (serve-yourself food) table?

5. Does your farm _____ (grow) organic _____ (farm products)?

6. Don't worry. He'll obey the commander. He's not a _____ (person who resists authority) and he won't _____ (rise to oppose you).

7. Even in the middle of a howling sandstorm, the loyal soldier would never _____ (abandon) his post in the _____ (dry, barren sandy land).

8. Every night she asks her dad to _____ (say printed words aloud) her the same story, even though he's _____ (rhymes with bed) it a million times.

The Ultimate Homework Book © 2008 by Marvin Terban, Scholastic Teaching Resources

SAME SPELL? OH, SWELL!

Homographs are words that are spelled the same but often sound different.

DIRECTIONS

Complete each sentence by choosing a word from the box below and writing a pair of homographs on the blank lines. Remember, the words will sound different and still fit the meaning of the sentence.

contest	polish	object	protest	moderate
content	wound	used	present	lead

1. After we shout "Happy Birthday!" we will _____ (give) him with the _____ (gift) we made.

2. Your honor, I _____ (disapprove of) to having that _____ (thing) introduced as evidence against my client.

3. He is a very _____ (reasonable; not extreme) person, so he was chosen to _____ (act as a moderator) the dispute.

4. He's the best singer in our school, so nobody will _____ (challenge) his winning the singing _____ (competition).

5. I _____ (regularly) to sell _____ (pre-owned) cars, but now I sell new ones.

6. I hope the people trying to sleep won't _____ (express an objection) too much when the noisy _____ (objection) march goes down the street.

7. I think I _____ (wrapped) the bandage around the _____ (injury) too loosely because it just fell off.

8. I asked the guide to _____ (show the way to) us to the gold mine, but he got lost and took us to the _____ (soft bluish-grey metal) mine instead.

9. I was exhausted trying to _____ (shine up) all that antique Italian, French, and _____ (from Poland) furniture.

10. I worked hard on my science report project, and the teacher was very _____ (satisfied) with its _____ (what was in it).

The Ultimate Homework Book © 2008 by Marvin Terban, Scholastic Teaching Resources

Homographs

SAME SPELL? WELL, WELL!

Homographs are words that are spelled the same but often sound different.

DIRECTIONS
Complete each sentence by choosing a word from the box below and writing a pair of homographs on the blank lines. Remember, the words will sound different and still fit the meaning of the sentence.

incense	wind	insult	refuse	drawer
convict	minute	shower	baton	subject

1. I'm a _____ (person who shows) of houses for sale, and what is amazing about this mansion is the computerized _____ (stand-up bath) in the bathroom.

2. I'm sorry but the town dump is full for today, and I must _____ (decline, turn down) any more _____ (garbage).

3. If her downstairs neighbor starts burning that smelly _____ , (sweet-smelling substance) it will _____ (make angry) her.

4. If the jury doesn't _____ (say he's guilty) him, he won't become a _____ (person in jail).

5. In _____ Rouge, Louisiana, the drum majorette did amazing tricks with her _____ (twirled stick).

6. In the study of what makes people laugh, we first _____ (force something on someone) the _____ (person being studied) to bad jokes, and then we tickle him with ostrich feathers.

7. In the top _____ (sliding storage box) of the art cabinet you'll find the drawings of our best _____ (person who draws).

8. It took me a good _____ (60 seconds) to see the dancing flea because it was so _____ (tiny).

9. It's very hard to _____ (wrap up) up the string on a kite when the _____ (strong breeze) is blowing so fiercely.

10. My angry brother tried to _____ (be rude to) me, but I wouldn't listen to his _____ (rude remark).

The Ultimate Homework Book © 2008 by Marvin Terban, Scholastic Teaching Resources

SAME SPELL? RINGS A BELL!

Homographs are words that are spelled the same but often sound different.

DIRECTIONS

Complete each sentence by choosing a word from the box below and writing a pair of homographs on the blank lines. Remember, the words will sound different and still fit the meaning of the sentence.

sewer	separate	row	do	perfect
house	project	number	live	progress

1. My favorite television program shows how people _____ (exist) in different parts of the world, and it's _____ (happening now, not recorded), not recorded on film or tape.

2. My gums kept getting _____ (less and less feeling) after the dentist injected Novocaine into them a _____ (certain amount) of times.

3. My music teacher tried to teach me how to sing "_____ (the first note on a scale) – re – mi," but I just couldn't _____ (accomplish) it.

4. My school's baseball team makes a little _____ (forward movement) every day as it tries to _____ (move forward) toward winning the state championship.

5. On the canoe, the brothers had a big _____ (quarrel) about who would be the first to _____ (paddle).

6. Please _____ (divide) the photos of animals into _____ (different) piles: vertebrates and invertebrates.

7. She thinks her violin playing isn't _____ (as good as possible) yet, so she practices five hours a day to _____ (make it as good as possible) it.

8. She was a _____ (stitcher) in a dress factory, and her husband worked underground in the _____ (waste tunnel).

9. Let's shut off the lights and _____ (show) a picture on the screen of how our grand _____ (enterprise, undertaking) will look when it's finished.

10. The army will _____ (provide shelter for) the soldiers in tents, but the general can stay in my _____ (home).

The Ultimate Homework Book © 2008 by Marvin Terban, Scholastic Teaching Resources

SAME SPELL? DO TELL!

Homographs are words that are spelled the same but often sound different.

DIRECTIONS
Complete each sentence by choosing a word from the box below and writing a pair of homographs on the blank lines. Remember, the words will sound different and still fit the meaning of the sentence.

dove	lives	putting	learned	bow
job	sow	entrance	estimate	primer

1. The beautiful princess's _____ (coming) into the ballroom will definitely _____ (fill with delight) all the people there.

2. The brilliant professor had _____ (acquired knowledge about) so many things, we called him "the _____ (wise and scholarly) man."

3. The farmer's daughter had to sew the clothes, _____ (scatter on the earth) the seeds, milk the cow, and feed the _____ (female pig).

4. The historian _____ (exists) for only one thing: to learn about the _____ (existences) of people in history.

5. The hungry _____ (bird of peace) _____ (dived) down and ate all the bird seed.

6. The man painting the classroom dribbled some paint _____ (paint for unpainted wall) on my favorite reading _____ (elementary, introductory textbook).

7. The new golfers were practicing on the _____ (smooth, grassy area for practicing golf swings) green, while the rest of us were _____ (placing) our golf clubs into the cart.

8. The plumber will _____ (roughly calculate) the cost of fixing your pipes and give you the _____ (rough calculation) before starting the job.

9. The prize-winning archer took a _____ (bend from the waist) after shooting an arrow from her _____ (arrow-shooting device) into the bull's eye.

10. The famous artist illustrated the Book of _____ (man in Bible story known for his patience) in the Bible, and she did a great _____ (piece of work).

The Ultimate Homework Book © 2008 by Marvin Terban, Scholastic Teaching Resources

SAME SPELLING? NO YELLING!

Homographs are words that are spelled the same but often sound different.

DIRECTIONS

Complete each sentence by choosing a word from the box below and writing a pair of homographs on the blank lines. Remember, the words will sound different and still fit the meaning of the sentence.

lima	record	herb	close	bass
peaked	evening	tear	tarry	permit

1. The runner's energy _____ (reached its highest point) at the tenth mile, then he felt a little _____ (worn out).

2. The singer with the _____ (lowest range) voice liked to fish for _____ (spiny-finned fish) in the sea.

3. They won't _____ (allow) me to fish here because I don't have a fishing _____ (official document saying it's OK to do something).

4. I ate the best _____ (flat, white bean) stew in my life in _____ (the capital city), Peru.

5. The workers paving the new road don't ever _____ (delay working). They worked quickly on their _____ (involving tar) job.

6. The world's leading expert on basil, parsley, oregano, and sage is Herbert Plantman, known as " _____ (short for "Herbert"), the _____ (plant used for flavoring) guy."

7. They spent the first _____ (early night) in their new house _____ (straightening) out all the crooked pictures on the walls.

8. When did the opera singer _____ (make sound permanent for replay later) the songs on this old phonograph _____ (a vinyl disk that plays recorded music)?

9. When she sees the _____ (rip) in her wedding gown, she'll certainly shed a _____ (drop of water from her eye) or two.

10. When you get _____ (near) to the barn, make sure to _____ (shut) the door so the horses won't get out.

The Ultimate Homework Book © 2008 by Marvin Terban, Scholastic Teaching Resources

SOUND-ALIKE WORDS

Homonyms are words that are spelled differently but sound alike. Sometimes they're called homophones. There are hundreds of pairs (sometimes triples) of homonyms. You see or hear them every day.

DIRECTIONS

Complete each sentence by choosing a word from the box below and writing it on the blank line(s). Another word in the same sentence is the hidden homonym of the word(s) you wrote. It will be pronounced exactly like that word or words, but it will be spelled differently. Find the hidden homonym and underline it. There are clues in parentheses to help you. Here's an example:

This <u>piece</u> of paper is the ___*peace*___ (opposite of war) treaty that ended the long war.

witch	foul	cents	too	sealing	bawled
two	threw	meat	ate	knight	scents

1. Good night, my good _____ (medieval soldier in armor).

2. That rotten fowl really smells _____ (awful).

3. Please tell me exactly which _____ (evil magical woman) you are.

4. It doesn't make sense to spend all those _____ (pennies) for those _____ (perfumes).

5. After his haircut, the man _____ (cried loudly) when he saw he was bald.

6. She went to _____ (between one and three) concerts _____ (also).

7. The butcher showed the vegetarian a sirloin steak and said, "I'd like you to meet some _____ (animal flesh)."

8. My little brother _____ (consumed food) all eight hot dogs by himself!

9. The pitcher _____ (propelled) the ball through the air amazingly fast.

10. There is a crack in my ceiling so the plasterer is up there _____ (filling in) it.

The Ultimate Homework Book © 2008 by Marvin Terban, Scholastic Teaching Resources

SOUNDS FAMILIAR

Homonyms are words that are spelled differently but sound alike. Sometimes they're called homophones. There are hundreds of pairs (sometimes triples) of homonyms. You see or hear them every day.

DIRECTIONS

Complete each sentence by choosing a word from the box below and writing it on the blank line(s). Another word in the same sentence is the hidden homonym of the word(s) you wrote. It will be pronounced exactly like that word or words, but it will be spelled differently. Find the hidden homonym and underline it. There are clues in parentheses to help you.

bee	hall	bare	they're	higher	
their	herd	sighed	brake	weather	pear

1. I _____ (let out a deep breath) sadly when I saw the dent in the side of my car.

2. The boss will hire me for a _____ (more high) position in the company.

3. When the _____ (group) of cattle heard all the noise, it started running.

4. Whether or not we have the picnic today will depend upon the _____ (atmospheric conditions).

5. I took only one pair of pants to wear and one ripe _____ (sweet, juicy fruit) to eat, and off I went.

6. You should try to break the habit of stepping on the _____ (stopping mechanism) so much.

7. A single _____ (buzzing, stinging insect) can be at only one flower at a time.

8. If the baby bear in the circus throws off its costume, will it be totally _____ (naked)?

9. _____ (they are) right over there in _____ (belongs to them) new car.

10. After the awards assembly, we will have to haul all the tables and chairs out of the _____ (area, room).

The Ultimate Homework Book © 2008 by Marvin Terban, Scholastic Teaching Resources

SOUNDS GOOD TO ME

Homonyms are words that are spelled differently but sound alike. Sometimes they're called homophones. There are hundreds of pairs (sometimes triples) of homonyms. You see or hear them every day.

DIRECTIONS
Complete each sentence by choosing a word from the box below and writing it on the blank line(s). Another word in the same sentence is the hidden homonym of the word(s) you wrote. It will be pronounced exactly like that word or words, but it will be spelled differently. Find the hidden homonym and underline it.

our	blue	flue	dye	due	made
lessen	dew	flour	serial	know	flu

1. Do you know when the morning _____ is _____ to burn off?

2. I just _____ you will say no to my idea, so I won't even tell you what it is.

3. The new maid had _____ the royal bed in a weird way, and the king couldn't get into it.

4. I was at home, sick with the _____ , when suddenly a bird flew down the chimney _____ and perched on my head.

5. She was eating her favorite cereal and watching the last program in a four-part _____ on dinosaurs when the electricity went out.

6. On _____ planet, an hour is 60 minutes, but what is it on other planets?

7. If you mixed petals from this edible flower into the _____ , you'll be able to bake Petunia Petal Pastries.

8. "If I _____ the homework," asked the teacher, "would that make the lesson more enjoyable for you, class?"

9. These beautiful flowers might die if you try to _____ them another color.

10. The dragon blew a cloud of _____ -colored smoke into the valley, and the ogre ran away.

The Ultimate Homework Book © 2008 by Marvin Terban, Scholastic Teaching Resources

SOUND OFF

Homonyms are words that are spelled differently but sound alike. Sometimes they're called homophones. There are hundreds of pairs (sometimes triples) of homonyms. You see or hear them every day.

DIRECTIONS

Complete each sentence by choosing a word from the box below and writing it on the blank line(s). Another word in the same sentence is the hidden homonym of the word(s) you wrote. It will be pronounced exactly like that word or words, but it will be spelled differently. Find the hidden homonym and underline it.

tale	feet	weight	male	steel	road
deer	rowed	minor	hole	paws	

1. Use the term *mail carrier* not *mailman* because the person could be female as well as _____ .

2. When my grandfather became a coal miner, he was just a _____ .

3. Oh look, dear, at that darling _____ behind the tree.

4. To walk on burning rocks in your bare _____ is quite an astonishing feat.

5. The manicurist had to pause and gasp when she saw the _____ of the lioness who wanted her nails cut and polished.

6. If you want to know your correct _____ you'll have to wait a minute because I have to fix the scale.

7. It took me a whole day to dig a _____ deep enough for a well.

8. The old seafarer told a marvelous _____ about the silver tail of the magical whale.

9. Did you really steal all that lumber and _____ to build your treehouse?

10. First he _____ his boat down the rushing river; then he rode his bike up the bumpy _____ to win the grand prize.

The Ultimate Homework Book © 2008 by Marvin Terban, Scholastic Teaching Resources

SOUNDS OK

Homonyms are words that are spelled differently but sound alike. Sometimes they're called homophones. There are hundreds of pairs (sometimes triples) of homonyms. You see or hear them every day.

DIRECTIONS

Complete each sentence by choosing a word from the box below to write on the lines. This homonym pair will be spelled differently but will sound the same. The sentences have to make sense when the blanks are filled in. Good luck!

dessert	sum	seas	beach	capitol	waste	seen
manners	pale	sale	beech	pail	some	
manors	sees	desert	sail	capital	scene	waist

1. From atop the lighthouse in the clouds, the ocean god _____ the seven _____ .

2. She filled the _____ with _____ pink paint and changed the color of her bedroom.

3. He's fantastic in math: He can add _____ numbers in his head and get the _____ without a calculator.

4. On this strict diet you will have to _____ the dinner table the moment _____ is served.

5. When you visit the _____ of British nobility, remember to use your best _____ .

6. I wasn't scared this time because I've _____ that _____ when the ghost jumps out of the closet in about a hundred other movies

7. Nothing grew on the lonely _____ except the _____ tree my grandfather planted at the spot where he had met my grandmother.

8. I know you want to lose some inches from your _____ , but you're still not allowed to _____ food in this house.

9. When you get to the state _____ , don't miss the tour of the _____ building.

10. Today I'm going to _____ my boat across the bay to the shopping mall because they're having a _____ on fishing poles.

The Ultimate Homework Book © 2008 by Marvin Terban, Scholastic Teaching Resources

SOUND-ALIKE TRIPLES

Homonyms are words that are spelled differently but sound alike. Sometimes they're called homophones. There are hundreds of pairs (sometimes triples) of homonyms. You see or hear them every day.

DIRECTIONS

Complete each sentence by choosing a word from the box below to write on the lines. The three words you write will be homonyms. They will be spelled differently but will sound the same. Some of these are really tricky, so keep a dictionary handy.

ewe	knew	rain	burrow	new	chord	Maine	cored	rays	for
eye	gnu	borough	rein	whey	four	weigh	raze	main	fore
raise	yew	mane	way	cord	reign	aye	you	burro	

1. "_____ ," said Captain Ahab, "_____ can see the whale with my one good _____ !"

2. In the _____ , a _____ tried to _____ a hole in the park.

3. At the zoo, they _____ that a brand _____ African antelope called a _____ was soon arriving.

4. I'll get a _____ in pay if I can _____ that ugly old boardwalk building and let more of the sun's _____ shine on the beach.

5. Little Miss Muffet knew the _____ to _____ her curds and _____ .

6. First I plugged in the _____ to my electric guitar, then I learned how to play a new _____ , and finally I _____ an apple for a snack.

7. Can _____ see the _____ that escaped from her flock standing in front of the _____ tree?

8. Whenever it would _____ during the _____ of King Timothy James I, the carriage driver would pull on a _____ and stop the horse.

9. The _____ thing you should see in the Portland, _____ , zoo is the miniature lion with the braided _____ .

10. One of the _____ golfers shouted, "_____ !" warning the other three to look out _____ the ball he was about to hit.

The Ultimate Homework Book © 2008 by Marvin Terban, Scholastic Teaching Resources

WELCOME TO THE IDIOM GYM

An idiom is a group of words with a special meaning. Often the individual words in the idiom don't relate to its meaning. There are lots of idioms that show action. They keep our language lively!

DIRECTIONS

Imagine you are the manager of the Idiom Gym. People come to exercise their favorite idioms. From the words in the box below, choose verbs to complete the idioms in the chart.

| beat | carry | climb | drive | hit | hold | jump | play |
| pull | run | scratch | sling | split | strike | tickle | |

IDIOM	MEANING
1. _____ **your leg**	to tease, fool, or lie to someone for a joke
2. _____ **the books**	to read, study, and do your homework
3. _____ **your funny bone**	make you laugh
4. _____ **while the iron is hot**	take action at the best time
5. _____ **hairs**	to argue about very minor details
6. _____ **around the bush**	avoid answering a question directly
7. _____ **the ball**	be in charge or responsible; do your fair share
8. _____ **your horses**	to wait a minute; be patient
9. _____ **the gun**	to start before you should
10. _____ **a hard bargain**	to demand hard terms when negotiating
11. _____ **the wall**	to be frustrated, anxious
12. _____ **hash**	work as a server in a restaurant that sells cheap food
13. _____ **second fiddle**	to be a follower; not to be the top person
14. _____ **the surface**	just starting to deal with something
15. _____ **circles around**	easily do something better than others

The Ultimate Homework Book © 2008 by Marvin Terban, Scholastic Teaching Resources

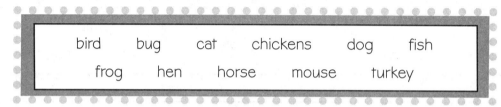

ANIMAL SAYINGS

An idiom is a group of words with a special meaning. Often the individual words in the idiom don't relate its meaning. There are many idioms that feature animals.

DIRECTIONS

Imagine that many animals from the land, air, and sea went on a picnic in Idiomland, but they got lost going home. See if you can put them back into the idioms they came from. From the words in the box below, choose animals to complete the sentences in the chart. Use each animal only once. There are 11 animals on the list but only 10 sentences, so one animal will not be used.

bird	bug	cat	chickens	dog	fish
frog	hen	horse	mouse	turkey	

IDIOM	MEANING
1. The **early** _____ **catches the worm.**	The person who starts a job first has the best chance of success.
2. **Don't count your** _____ **before they hatch.**	Don't count on something good happening before it does.
3. **Don't look a gift** _____ **in the mouth.**	Don't ask questions about the value of a gift someone's giving you.
4. **Don't let the** _____ **out of the bag.**	Don't tell a secret.
5. She has **a** _____ **in her throat.**	a hoarse voice
6. He loves **the** _____ **days of summer.**	the hottest days of summer, in July and August
7. The sleeping baby was **as quiet as a** _____ .	very, very quiet
8. The businesswomen are **talking** _____ .	discussing business
9. The angry principal was **as mad as a wet** _____ .	extremely angry
10. Now this is **a pretty kettle of** _____ .	in a big mess; in trouble

The Ultimate Homework Book © 2008 by Marvin Terban, Scholastic Teaching Resources

PUT THE ANIMALS INTO THEIR SAYINGS

An idiom is a group of words with a special meaning. Often the individual words in the idiom don't relate to its meaning. There are many idioms that feature animals.

DIRECTIONS

From the words in the box below, choose animals to complete the sentences in the chart. Use each animal only once. There are 12 animals on the list but only 11 blank lines, so one animal will not be used.

| beaver | bull | fox | goose | lamb | leopard |
| monkey | pigeon | possum | rat | sheep | wolf |

IDIOM	MEANING
1. I think I **smell a** _____ .	suspect something is wrong or dishonest
2. He's **as clumsy as a** _____ **in a china shop**.	very clumsy
3. He's a _____ **in** _____ **'s clothing**.	to pretend to be nice, but to really be a bad person
4. I'll be there in **two shakes of a** _____ **'s tale**.	very quickly
5. It was **a wild** _____ **chase**.	made you look foolish
6. The little kid was just **playing** _____ .	pretending to be asleep
7. She's a real **eager** _____ .	enthusiastic, hard-working person
8. They **made a** _____ **out of you!**	made you look foolish
9. A _____ **can't change its spots**.	a person's basic nature and habits can't change
10. That **stool** _____ told everything he knew.	an informer

The Ultimate Homework Book © 2008 by Marvin Terban, Scholastic Teaching Resources

ANIMAL EXPRESSIONS

An idiom is a group of words with a special meaning. Often the individual words in the idiom don't relate to its meaning. There are many idioms that feature animals.

DIRECTIONS

From the words in the box below, choose animals to complete the sentences in the chart. Use each animal only once. There are 12 animals on the list but only 11 sentences, so one animal will not be used.

| ants | bug | butterflies | crow | fly | grasshopper |
| hornet | moth | peacock | snail | snake | whale |

IDIOM	MEANING
1. He hates to **eat** _____ , but he had to.	admit you're wrong
2. She is **as proud as a** _____ .	very proud of oneself; vain; conceited
3. There's **a** _____ **in the ointment.**	a small problem
4. Be careful not to **stir up a** _____ **'s nest.**	cause a lot of trouble
5. When I got up to speak, I **had** _____ **in my stomach.**	to feel very nervous
6. My little brother **has** _____ **in his pants.**	one who fidgets, can't sit still, is very restless
7. Hurry up! You're walking at **a** _____ **'s pace.**	very slowly
8. I remember you when you were **knee-high to a** _____ .	very young and small
9. Don't trust him. He's **a** _____ **in the grass.**	dishonest and evil in a sneaky way
10. She was **as snug as a** _____ **in a rug.**	very comfy and cozy

The Ultimate Homework Book © 2008 by Marvin Terban, Scholastic Teaching Resources

THE IDIOM CLOTHING STORE

An idiom is a group of words with a special meaning. Often the individual words in the idiom don't relate to its meaning.

Have you heard the famous old saying, "Clothes make the man"? Of course, they make the woman, too!

DIRECTIONS

Imagine you are the owner of an idiom clothing store. A shipment of clothing idioms has just arrived, along with signs telling what they mean. From the words in the box below, choose articles of clothing to complete the idoms in the chart.

| belt | britches | cap | collar | gloves |
| pants | shirt | shoe | shoestring | sleeve |

IDIOM	MEANING
1. feather in your _____	a great achievement; something to be proud of
2. fly by the seat of your _____	do something without really knowing what you're doing
3. give someone the _____ off your back	to be extremely generous
4. handle with kid _____	to treat a person or situation very carefully and gently
5. hit below the _____	to use unfair tactics; to be unsportsmanlike
6. hot under the _____	upset and very angry
7. wear your heart on your _____	openly show your emotions
8. on a _____	using very little money; on a strict budget
9. too big for your _____	conceited; full of self-importance
10. If the _____ fits, wear it.	to admit when someone says something about you that's true

The Ultimate Homework Book © 2008 by Marvin Terban, Scholastic Teaching Resources

EXPRESS YOURSELF WITH COLOR

An idiom is a group of words with a special meaning. Often the individual words in the idiom don't relate to its meaning.

Don't you think the world would be an awfully drab place without colors? Maybe that's why so many idioms contain the names of colors in them.

DIRECTIONS

Show your true colors by getting six colored pencils, markers, or crayons (blue, black, silver, red, green, and pink). To complete the sentences in the chart, write the words **blue**, **black**, **silver**, **red**, **green**, or **pink** on the blank lines. Be sure to use the appropriate color of pencil, marker, or crayon.

IDIOM	MEANING
1. between the devil and the deep _____ sea	between two difficult and dangerous positions
2. _____ sheep of the family	the worst member of a good family
3. _____ blood	of high birth; from the upper class of society
4. _____-letter day	a very important, memorable day
5. bolt from the _____	something very unexpected
6. born with a _____ spoon in your mouth	born wealthy
7. catch someone _____-handed	catch someone in the middle of doing something wrong
8. have a _____ thumb	able to make plants and flowers grow
9. in the _____	extremely healthy
10. _____ with envy	extremely jealous
11. _____ herring	something deliberately misleading
12. tickled _____	amused, pleased, delighted
13. _____ tape	rules and regulations that slow things down
14. _____-carpet treatment	special treatment for important people
15. true _____	very loyal

The Ultimate Homework Book © 2008 by Marvin Terban, Scholastic Teaching Resources

TASTY SAYINGS

An idiom is a group of words with a special meaning. Often the individual words in the idiom don't relate to its meaning.

Do you ever wonder why so many idioms contain the names of foods? Maybe it's because if we didn't eat, we couldn't live.

DIRECTIONS

Imagine you're the manager of an idiom food shop. A truckload of fresh food has just arrived. You have to put all the foods into their idioms. From the words in the box below, choose foods to complete the idioms in the chart.

| apple | banana | beans | butter | cake | cookie | cucumber |
| egg | salt | peas | pickle | pie | pudding | fruitcake |

IDIOM	MEANING
1. _____ of your eye	a person or a thing that is very much loved
2. _____ someone up	to flatter someone
3. cool as a _____	very calm; not nervous
4. easy as _____	extremely easy
5. _____ on your face	embarrassed about something you did
6. worth your _____	deserved your pay
7. have your _____ and eat it too	to have two things when you're supposed to choose only one
8. in a _____	in big trouble
9. like two _____ in a pod	exactly alike
10. nutty as a _____	totally crazy
11. proof of the _____ is in the eating	final result proves how successful something is
12. spill the _____	reveal a secret
13. that's the way the _____ crumbles	the way life is, and you can't do anything about it
14. top _____	the star comedian in a show; the boss

The Ultimate Homework Book © 2008 by Marvin Terban, Scholastic Teaching Resources

HATS OFF TO IDIOMS!

An idiom is a group of words with a special meaning. Often the individual words in the idiom don't relate to its meaning.

There are more idioms about hats than about practically any other single thing. Maybe that's because hats are the clothing we wear closest to our brains!

DIRECTIONS
Match the meanings below to the hat idioms.

MEANINGS

1. to produce a needed thing as if by magic

2. to ask for contributions of money

3. to talk nonsense; to not know what you're saying

4. to keep a secret

5. to announce that you're running for election to an office

6. to act humbly; to beg for a favor

7. old-fashioned; out-of-date

8. to praise a person for a great accomplishment

9. something you say when you're 100 percent positive you're right, and this is what you'll do if you're wrong

10. immediately; without delay; at once

1. keep something under your **hat**   Meaning # _____

2. **hat** in hand   Meaning # _____

3. old **hat**   Meaning # _____

4. pass the **hat**   Meaning # _____

5. pull a rabbit out of a **hat**   Meaning # _____

6. take off your **hat** to someone   Meaning # _____

7. talk through your **hat**   Meaning # _____

8. throw your **hat** into the ring   Meaning # _____

9. at the drop of a **hat**   Meaning # _____

10. I'll eat my **hat**   Meaning # _____

The Ultimate Homework Book © 2008 by Marvin Terban, Scholastic Teaching Resources

BODY SAYINGS

An idiom is a group of words with a special meaning. Often the individual words in the idiom don't relate to its meaning.

Have you ever noticed that many idioms have parts of bodies in them? Maybe that's because we're surrounded by them!

DIRECTIONS

Imagine you own a store that supplies body parts for robots, statues, department store mannequins, and idioms. A sudden strong wind has blown all the body parts off their shelves. Now it's your job to put them back into their rightful idioms. Do it by completing the chart below with words from the box. Hint: One word is used twice.

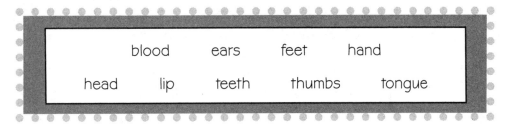

| blood | ears | feet | hand |
| head | lip | teeth | thumbs | tongue |

IDIOM	MEANING
1. all _____	listening eagerly
2. all _____	very clumsy and awkward with your hands
3. bite your _____	to force yourself not to say something; take back what you've already said
4. bite the _____ that feeds you	to turn against someone who helps you
5. _____ is thicker than water	to expect more from a relative than a non-relative
6. bury your _____ in the sand	to ignore danger by pretending you don't see it
7. button your _____	to be quiet; stop talking
8. keep a stiff upper _____	to show bravery in the face of troubles
9. by the skin of your _____	just barely; very, very close
10. cold _____	a fear of doing something

The Ultimate Homework Book © 2008 by Marvin Terban, Scholastic Teaching Resources

BODY LANGUAGE

An idiom is a group of words with a special meaning. Often the individual words in the idiom don't relate to its meaning.

Have you ever noticed that many idioms have parts of bodies in them? Maybe that's because we're surrounded by them!

DIRECTIONS
Complete the chart below with words from the box. Hint: One word is used four times.

chest	elbow	eyes	face	hand	head	heart
mouth	heels	nail	nose	shoulders	skin	throat	tooth

IDIOM	MEANING
1. cut off your _____ to spite your _____	to harm yourself spitefully because you're angry with someone else
2. _____ grease	hard manual labor
3. _____ In the back of your _____	ability to know what's happening without seeing it
4. fight _____ and _____	to fight fiercely
5. get something off your _____	to tell what's bothering you
6. get under your _____	to upset or bother you greatly
7. _____-to-_____ existence	to spend all that you earn without saving any money
8. _____ and _____ above someone	much better at something than someone else
9. _____ in the clouds	lost in thought; absentminded; not paying attention
10. _____ over _____ in love	completely and helplessly in love
11. _____ is in the right place	to be kindhearted and well-meaning
12. jump down your _____	to scream at someone angrily for something

The Ultimate Homework Book © 2008 by Marvin Terban, Scholastic Teaching Resources

BODY TALK

An idiom is a group of words with a special meaning. Often the individual words in the idiom don't relate to its meaning.

Have you ever noticed that many idioms have parts of bodies in them? Maybe that's because we're surrounded by them!

DIRECTIONS
Complete the chart below with words from the box. Hint: Two words are used more than once.

| ear | eyes | finger | foot | hair | heels | neck | nose |

IDIOM	MEANING
1. keep your _____ to the ground	to pay attention and know what's going on
2. keep your _____ to the grindstone	to work hard all the time
3. kick up your _____	to have a wonderful time; enjoy yourself
4. let your _____ down	to relax and behave freely and naturally
5. look down your _____ at someone	to treat people as if they were lower in quality than you
6. need something like a hole in the _____	to have no need for something at all
7. pay through the _____	to pay way too much money for something
8. pull the wool over your _____	to cheat or fool someone
9. put your best _____ forward	to do your best to make the best impression
10. put your _____ on something	to identify something exactly
11. put your _____ down	to be firm or unyielding about something
12. albatross around your _____	a difficult burden you can't get rid of

The Ultimate Homework Book © 2008 by Marvin Terban, Scholastic Teaching Resources

I GOTTA HAND IT TO YOU!

An idiom is a group of words with a special meaning. Often the individual words in the idiom don't relate to its meaning.

Have you ever noticed that many idioms have parts of bodies in them? Maybe that's because we're surrounded by them!

DIRECTIONS
Complete the chart below with words from the box. Hint: One word is used twice.

| cheek | elbows | eye | eyebrow | eyes | feet | head |
| heel | leg | neck | shoulder | tongue | tooth |

IDIOM	MEANING
1. raise an _____	to shock or surprise people by doing something outrageous
2. rub _____ with someone	to be in the same place and meet people
3. see _____ to _____	to agree; to have the same opinion about something
4. shake a _____	to speed up; go faster
5. sight for sore _____	a pleasant, unexpected, and welcome sight
6. stick your _____ out	to do something risky that people could criticize you for
7. sweep you off your _____	to make a very favorable impression on someone; to make someone love you quickly
8. have a sweet _____	a great desire to eat sugary foods
9. _____-in-_____	meant as a joke; not to be taken seriously
10. Achilles' _____	the one weakness in something otherwise good or strong
11. chip on your _____	quarrelsome, rude, aggressive; ready to fight
12. keep your _____ above water	to earn enough money to pay your bills

The Ultimate Homework Book © 2008 by Marvin Terban, Scholastic Teaching Resources

YIPPEE! I FOUND AN INTERJECTION!

An interjection is a word (sometimes two words) that shows an emotion or feeling like surprise, horror, disgust, happiness, shock, etc. An interjection almost always comes at the beginning of a sentence.

If the emotion is very strong, put an exclamation point after it:

> **Yikes!** A little mouse just ran up my pants.

If the emotion or feeling is not too strong, just a comma will do:

> **Oh,** I didn't know this mustache was yours.

Here are some common interjections you might hear, read, or say:

- **Wow!**
- **Gadzooks!**
- **Hey,**
- **Good grief,**
- **Yippee!**
- **Gee whiz,**
- **Well,**
- **All right,**

You can even make up your own interjections, if you want to. Just make sure they fit the feeling of the sentence:

> **Leaping lizards!** You almost painted my toenails blue, Louise.

DIRECTIONS

In each sentence below, underline the interjection, including the punctuation that follows it.

1. Whoa! Calm down and don't get so excited. I can fix this with gum.

2. Alas, dear Chester, the flowers have wilted in the hot sun.

3. Mmm, this chocolate chip peanut butter cookie tastes great.

4. Aha! Now I know which gerbil ate the birdseed.

5. Gosh, that's an awfully small costume for a giant.

6. Help! My nose is caught in the pencil sharpener!

7. Uh-oh, I think the teacher is going to give us a surprise quiz.

8. Yuck! This beef stew you made tastes like dog food.

9. Phew, I'm glad the snow stopped falling before the concert.

10. Ouch! I think I just sat on Grandma's prize cactus plant.

The Ultimate Homework Book © 2008 by Marvin Terban, Scholastic Teaching Resources

YIKES! COMMA OR EXCLAMATION MARK?

An interjection is a word (sometimes two words) that shows an emotion or feeling like surprise, horror, disgust, happiness, shock, etc. An interjection almost always comes at the beginning of a sentence.

DIRECTIONS

In the sentences below, the interjections are all in boldface. After each interjection, put a comma if you think the emotion being expressed is mild or an exclamation mark if you think it's strong.

TiPS

- If you put in an exclamation mark, remember to change the first letter of the next word to a capital letter and put another exclamation mark or period at the end of the sentence.

- If you put in a comma, don't capitalize the next word. Remember to put a period at the end of the sentence.

1. **Hooray** we just won the championships for the first time in history

2. **Oops** he just spilled a little milk, but I won't cry over it

3. **Eek** that's not a rubber rat. It's a real one

4. **Darn** there's a hole in my stocking

5. **Ugh** somebody put gooey green slime in my sneakers

6. **Well** we have to feed the rabbits before we paint the kitchen

7. **Gee** it's almost five o'clock

8. **Bravo** you're the greatest opera singer in the world

9. **All right** class, let's open our books to page 23

10. **Whoopee** I just found the five dollars I was looking for

The Ultimate Homework Book © 2008 by Marvin Terban, Scholastic Teaching Resources

CREATE YOUR OWN INTERJECTIONS

An interjection is a word (sometimes two words) that shows an emotion or feeling like surprise, horror, disgust, happiness, shock, etc. An interjection almost always comes at the beginning of a sentence.

DIRECTIONS

Read each sentence below carefully. Make up your own one- or two-word interjection for it. Make sure it fits the mood of the sentence that follows it. On the blank line in front of every sentence, write your original interjection. After it, put a comma or exclamation point to show if it's mild or strong.

TiPS

- If you put in an exclamation mark, change the first letter of the next word to a capital letter and put another exclamation mark or a period at the end of the sentence.

- If you put in a comma, don't capitalize the next word. Remember to put a period at the end of the sentence.

1. _____ my cat just had eight kittens

2. _____ this hat doesn't go with my suit

3. _____ a stampede of elephants is coming

4. _____ this soup isn't hot enough

5. _____ it's starting to drizzle

6. _____ the volcano is erupting

7. _____ we've run out of chips for the party

8. _____ my dog ate my science project

9. _____ this button is the perfect color

10. _____ the tiger has escaped from its cage

The Ultimate Homework Book © 2008 by Marvin Terban, Scholastic Teaching Resources

NOUNS ABOUND!

Nouns are very important words because they name all the persons, places, things, and ideas (feelings or qualities) in the world. There are more nouns in English than any other kind of word. Here are some examples for each category:

PERSONS	PLACES	THINGS	IDEAS
teacher	forest	pencil	freedom
brother	village	football	pleasure

DIRECTIONS

All the nouns in the sentences below are in boldface. Over the nouns, write **PER** if they name persons, **PL** if they name places, **TH** if they name things, or **ID** if they name ideas.

Note: Some people would put animals in the person category. Other people categorize them as things. What do you think? If a noun below names an animal, you can put it in either category.

1. The **painter** found her **shoe** in the **studio** but lost her **feathers**.

2. At **college** the **professor** teaches the **students** about **justice** and **honesty**.

3. In the **store** in the **hotel**, a **man** sold **candy**, **newspapers**, and **gum**.

4. My **family** took a **trip** to **Italy** and went to many **castles** and **cathedrals**.

5. My **aunt** loves **animals**, and once had three **dogs**, two **cats**, and a **ferret**.

6. **Lorrie** got **tomatoes**, a **lemon**, and a **bunch** of **bananas** at the **market**.

7. The **citizens** of **France** fought for **liberty**, **fraternity**, and **equality**.

8. Take **boots**, a **coat**, **gloves**, a **hat**, and a **scarf** for the **hike** in the **woods**.

9. In the **city** the **kids** saw **plays** and went to **museums**.

10. My **sister** took a **computer** and **printer** to **school** but forgot the **cables**.

The Ultimate Homework Book © 2008 by Marvin Terban, Scholastic Teaching Resources

ONE OR MORE?

Nouns are very important words because they name all the persons, places, things, and ideas (feelings or qualities) in the world.

There are several different kinds of nouns. One kind is singular and another kind is plural. Singular means one person, place, thing, or idea. Plural means more than one. Here are some examples:

SINGULAR	telephone	printer	lollipop	textbook
PLURAL	telephones	printers	lollipops	textbooks

Regular nouns, such as the ones above, just add the letter **s** to the singular spelling to make it plural.

DIRECTIONS

In the following sentences, underline all the nouns you find. Then print a capital **S** over all the singular nouns and a capital **P** over all the plural nouns. There are a total of 46 nouns in these sentences.

1. The singer sang songs from two operas in the talent show at the school.

2. The man who grows flowers sent me a rose and some daffodils.

3. Mix in three eggs, a stick of butter, and a lemon for flavor.

4. Pack your new shirt, socks, a belt, handkerchiefs, and your toothbrush.

5. If you cross the street and walk two blocks, you'll come to the ballpark.

6. The stories the students read in the green book were great.

7. A monkey at the zoo threw peanuts at my cousins from Chicago.

8. The clowns at the circus wore funny noses, big shoes, and crazy hats.

9. The teacher told the boy to take the pencils to the office of the principal.

10. At the aquarium my friend saw sharks, a whale, guppies, and his dad.

The Ultimate Homework Book © 2008 by Marvin Terban, Scholastic Teaching Resources

PECULIAR PLURALS

Nouns are very important words because they name all the persons, places, things, and ideas (feelings or qualities) in the world.

There are several different kinds of nouns. One kind is singular and another kind is plural. Singular means one person, place, thing, or idea. Plural means more than one. Here are some examples:

SINGULAR	lady	foot	knife	child
PLURAL	ladies	feet	knives	children

Irregular plural nouns, such as the ones above, don't just add **s** to the singular spellings to become plural. They change their spellings in different ways.

DIRECTIONS

On the blank lines in each sentence, write the plural spelling of the noun in boldface. This can be tricky because some nouns don't change at all, and some may have more than one correct plural spelling. You might want to consult your favorite dictionary if you get stuck.

1. First I heard one **goose** honking; then I heard a flock of _____ .

2. The saleslady sold a hat to one **woman** and coats to four _____ .

3. A **deer** ran by us in the woods followed by six other _____ .

4. I ate one **half** of my cupcake; my sister ate both _____ of hers.

5. Don't worry, Mom. I broke one back **tooth**, not two front _____ .

6. I'm just one **alumnus** of this college. There are many other _____ .

7. I left a piece of cheese for my **mouse**, and several _____ came to eat it.

8. There's no **octopus** in this tank, but five _____ are in that one.

9. This **ox** can't pull the cart himself, so hitch up both _____ .

10. I watch one **baby** on weekdays and three _____ on weekends.

The Ultimate Homework Book © 2008 by Marvin Terban, Scholastic Teaching Resources

HOW COMMON! HOW PROPER!

Nouns are very important words because they name all the persons, places, things, and ideas (feelings or qualities) in the world.

Some nouns are common and some are proper. Common means any person, place, or thing. Proper means a specific person, place, or thing. Here are some examples:

	PERSONS	PLACES	THINGS
COMMON	farmer	school	toothpaste
PROPER	Mr. Agricola	Columbia Prep	Crest

Proper nouns always begin with capital letters. They can also be more than one word: Empire State Building, Golden Gate Bridge, John F. Kennedy, General Electric

TiP

Nouns that name ideas can sometimes be proper nouns, but usually only in songs or poems, like this:

Oh, Freedom, come touch me with your hands.

So I can seek Happiness in better lands.

DIRECTIONS
In the following sentences, underline all the nouns. Then print a capital **C** over all the common nouns and a capital **P** over all the proper nouns. There are a total of 47 nouns in these sentences.

1. Of all the cities on the planet Earth, I like Rome and Barcelona the best.

2. David climbed many mountains before Everest and Kilimanjaro.

3. Rachel's mom loved seeing the Taj Mahal in India and Masada in Israel.

4. Gribbet is the name of my frog; Hopper is the name of my rabbit.

5. Houdini, a famous magician born in Hungary, did astounding tricks.

6. He has a laptop, a printer, and a cell from, respectively, Apple, Brother, and Nokia.

7. Harriet Tubman is a very important woman in the history of America.

8. Which is the longest river in the world: the Amazon or the Nile?

The Ultimate Homework Book © 2008 by Marvin Terban, Scholastic Teaching Resources

HAVE "PRIDE" IN YOUR "SCHOOL"

A group of animals may be called by many different names, depending on the animals. For example, a group of lions is called a pride (which should make them very proud). A group of fish is called a school (which should make them very smart).

DIRECTIONS

The list below contains the names of many different animal groupings. Match the group name to the animals by filling in the blanks with words from the list. If you get stuck, your friendly dictionary will help you.

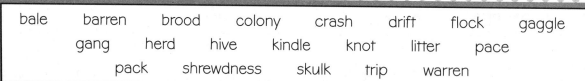

bale	barren	brood	colony	crash	drift	flock	gaggle
gang	herd	hive	kindle	knot	litter	pace
pack	shrewdness	skulk	trip	warren

A GROUP OF . . .   IS CALLED A . . .

1. ants _____
2. apes _____
3. bees _____
4. buffalo _____
5. cattle _____
6. chickens _____
7. dogs _____
8. donkeys _____
9. foxes _____
10. geese _____
11. hogs _____
12. kittens _____
13. mules _____
14. puppies _____
15. rabbits _____
16. rhinoceroses _____
17. seals _____
18. sheep _____
19. toads _____
20. turtles _____

The Ultimate Homework Book © 2008 by Marvin Terban, Scholastic Teaching Resources

THE SUBJECT FOR TODAY IS NOUNS

Nouns are very important words because they name all the persons, places, things, and ideas (feelings or qualities) in the world. Here are some examples for each category:

PERSONS	PLACES	THINGS	IDEAS
pilot	store	book	mercy
father	restaurant	computer	goodness

Nouns can be used in many different ways in a sentence. One use of a noun is as the subject of the sentence. Every sentence must have a subject. You can always identify the subject in these two ways:

1. The subject is who or what the sentence is mainly about.

2. The subject is the noun that performs the action of the verb.

For example:

My sister found the lost dog.

Who found the lost dog? My sister. Who is this sentence mainly about? My sister. **Sister** is the subject of the sentence.

DIRECTIONS

In the following sentences underline all the subjects. Hint: Find the verb (action word) first. Then ask yourself, "Who or what is doing or did this?" The answer will be the subject.

1. Last night my neighbor taught his cat how to whistle through its teeth.

2. Unfortunately, the principal canceled the picnic because of the snow.

3. A tiny snake slithered out from under a branch near my sister's shoe.

4. After three weeks the company sent me an e-mail with the instructions.

5. At the circus the ringmaster announces all the acts in a booming voice.

6. My 5-year-old cousin learns French from a computer program.

7. Dennis loves Lynda's cooking, especially her Scottish dishes.

8. My friend from London wrote a book about the Civil War.

9. Isla watches her brother Andrew for two hours every Saturday.

10. At the diner, the waitress brought us free sodas with our meals.

The Ultimate Homework Book © 2008 by Marvin Terban, Scholastic Teaching Resources

WHAT'S THE OBJECT OF THIS?

Nouns are very important words because they name all the persons, places, things, and ideas (feelings or qualities) in the world. Here are some examples for each category:

PERSONS	PLACES	THINGS	IDEAS
soldier	desert	lamp	honesty
governor	meadow	camera	friendship

Nouns can be used many different ways in a sentence. One use of a noun is as the direct object of the sentence. The direct object is the noun that receives the action of the verb. For example:

> My sister found the lost dog.

What is the verb (the word that shows action)? Found. What did my sister find? The dog. **Dog** is the direct object. The dog didn't perform any action in this sentence. It received an action. It was found.

DIRECTIONS

In the following sentences underline the direct objects. Not every sentence in English has a direct object, but all the sentences on this page do. Hint: First find the verb. Ask yourself, "Who is receiving the action of this verb?" The answer will be the direct object.

1. Shakespeare wrote many famous plays around the year 1600.

2. The pitcher threw the ball to the catcher at 93 miles per hour.

3. My grandfather baked my grandmother a chocolate cream pie.

4. Charles Lindbergh flew a plane from Long Island, New York, to Paris in 1927.

5. Mrs. Williams corrected our English tests over the weekend.

6. Tim's dog ate all the meatballs while we were swimming in the pool.

7. For six years in a row my school won the state basketball championship.

8. I saw Mount Rushmore from a helicopter flying over the site.

9. My sister likes scary movies with funny stories.

10. In the final game, my father hit a home run way over the fence.

The Ultimate Homework Book © 2008 by Marvin Terban, Scholastic Teaching Resources

POOF! YOU'RE A NOUN!

Nouns are very important words because they name all the persons, places, things, and ideas (feelings or qualities) in the world.

A suffix is a group of letters added to the end of a word. Some suffixes turn adjectives (words that describe nouns) and verbs (words that show action) into nouns. For example:

WORD	+ SUFFIX	= NOUN
free (adjective)	+ dom	= freedom
creative (adjective)	+ ity	= creativity
celebrate (verb)	+ tion	= celebration
fight (verb)	+ er	= fighter
act (verb)	+ or	= actor
active (adjective)	+ ist	= activist
dark (adjective)	+ ness	= darkness

DIRECTIONS

Add the suffix in the second column to the word in the first column to make a noun. Write the noun in the third column. You may have to adjust the spelling. Check with a dictionary to make sure of the correct spelling of the noun.

VERB or ADJECTIVE	+ SUFFIX	= NOUN
1. bore	+ dom	=
2. wise	+ dom	=
3. equal	+ ity	=
4. real	+ ity	=
5. permit	+ sion	=
6. discuss	+ sion	=
7. educate	+ tion	=
8. imagine	+ tion	=
9. achieve	+ er	=
10. challenge	+ er	=
11. direct	+ or	=
12. illustrate	+ or	=
13. tour	+ ist	=
14. final	+ ist	=
15. attractive	+ ness	=
16. busy	+ ness	=

The Ultimate Homework Book © 2008 by Marvin Terban, Scholastic Teaching Resources

MOO! GOBBLE! AND HONK!

Onomatopoeia is the use of words that imitate sounds. Animals make a lot of sounds.

DIRECTIONS

From the list of words below, choose the sounds that best complete the story.

baaing	barking	bleating	braying	buzzing	chattering	chirping
clucking	croaking	gobbling	honking	hooting	howling	meowing
mooing	neighing	oinking	quacking	roaring	squeaking	trumpeting

Listen to the Animals Talking

After taking a course in animal sounds in college, my older brother could identify sounds I wasn't even aware of. One day he took me for a walk to demonstrate his new skills.

"Can you hear the _____ of that **bee**?" he asked. "If you hear it before you see it, you can get out of its way before it stings you."

Then he pointed up to a tree. "Isn't the _____ of those **birds** lovely? It's very different from the _____ of the **owl** in the next tree."

As we passed a farm he pointed out the _____ of the **cows**, the _____ of a **donkey**, the _____ of the **pigs**, the _____ of a **goat**, and the _____ of some **sheep**.

"I hear the _____ of the **chickens**, the _____ of a **turkey**, and the _____ of a **horse**," I shouted.

Near a little pond, I called out, "Listen to the _____ of the **ducks**, the _____ of the **frogs**, and the _____ of the **geese**."

"You're getting to be an animal sound expert," my brother said to me.

We entered the zoo, and immediately my ears were bombarded by all the sounds around me: the _____ of the **elephants**, the _____ of the **lions**, the _____ of the **wolves**, and the _____ of the **monkeys**.

Back home, the _____ of my **cat** and the _____ of the neighbor's **dog** sounded beautiful. Even the _____ of my pet **mouse** was music to my ears.

The Ultimate Homework Book © 2008 by Marvin Terban, Scholastic Teaching Resources

HELLO, PAL!

A palindrome is a word that is the same read backward or forward.

DIRECTIONS
From the list below, choose words to write on the blank lines. The words are all palindromes. They go backward and forward.

bib	dad	deed	did	eye	ewe	kayak
level	ma'am	madam	mom	noon	nun	

1. A father is a _____ .

2. A mother is a _____ .

3. The organ that you see with is your _____ .

4. An Eskimo canoe is a _____ .

5. Twelve o'clock in the daytime is _____ .

6. A noble or brave act is a good _____ .

7. What keeps a baby's clothes clean when it eats is a _____ .

8. A short way of saying "Madam" is _____ .

9. Something flat, even, and horizontal is _____ .

10. The past tense of the verb "to do" is _____ .

11. A woman who is a member of a religious community is a _____ .

12. A female sheep is a _____ .

13. A way to address a woman politely and respectfully is _____ .

The Ultimate Homework Book © 2008 by Marvin Terban, Scholastic Teaching Resources

MY PALS AND I

A palindrome is a word that is the same read backward or forward.

DIRECTIONS
From the list below, choose words to write on the blank lines. The words are all palindromes. They go backward and forward.

peep	pup	radar	redder	reviver	rotor
shahs	sis	solos	toot	tot	Tut

1. The sound of a tin horn is a _____ .

2. A little dog is a _____ .

3. The sound of a little bird is a _____ .

4. A sister is a _____ .

5. An Egyptian boy king was named _____ .

6. A device for tracking aircraft is _____ .

7. A very young child is a _____ .

8. Part of a machine that turns round and round is a _____ .

9. Songs sung by one person are _____ .

10. Former leaders of Iran were once called _____ .

11. More red is _____ .

12. A person who revives you is a _____ .

The Ultimate Homework Book © 2008 by Marvin Terban, Scholastic Teaching Resources

FLIP-FLOPS

Sometimes you can take a word, reverse its letters, and make another word. For example, **pot** flipped backwards is **top**. **Pot top** is a two-word palindrome. Read it backwards and it's still **pot top**. If you wanted to make up a riddle that has **pot top** as the answer, you might ask:

"What do you call the lid of a cooking utensil?" Answer: Pot top!

PART 1

DIRECTIONS
First, flip the letters of the words at right to make new words. Write those words on the blank lines.

FLIP-FLOPS

1. bag _____   6. pan _____
2. lap _____   7. pit _____
3. live _____   8. snug _____
4. mad _____   9. swap _____
5. pals _____   10. won _____

PART 2

DIRECTIONS
Now match the two-word palindromes from Part 1 to the riddles below.

1. What is an angry wall that holds back water?   **Flip-Flop # _____**

2. What do you call the very top of a ditch?   **Flip-Flop # _____**

3. What are pistols in holsters that are too small?   **Flip-Flop # _____**

4. What kind of friend sits on you and snuggles?   **Flip-Flop # _____**

5. What does the devil want people to do?   **Flip-Flop # _____**

6. You came in first in a race this minute. What did you do?   **Flip-Flop # _____**

7. When dogs trade hands, what do they do?   **Flip-Flop # _____**

8. When a frying dish sleeps, what do you call it?   **Flip-Flop # _____**

9. What do friends do when they hit each other?   **Flip-Flop # _____**

10. What do you call paper container chatter?   **Flip-Flop # _____**

The Ultimate Homework Book © 2008 by Marvin Terban, Scholastic Teaching Resources

FLIP 'EM BACKWARD

Sometimes you can take a word, reverse its letters, and make another word. For example, **pot** flipped backwards is **top**. **Pot top** is a two-word palindrome. Read it backwards and it's still **pot top**. If you wanted to make up a riddle that has **pot top** as the answer, you might ask:

"What do you call the lid of a cooking utensil?" Answer: Pot top!

PART 1

DIRECTIONS
First, flip the letters of the words at right to make new words. Write those words on the blank lines.

FLIP-FLOPS

1. bad _____
2. dog _____
3. bus _____
4. cod _____
5. gum _____

6. rats _____
7. tap _____
8. straw _____
9. pets _____
10. net _____

PART 2

DIRECTIONS
Now match the two-word palindromes from Part 1 to the riddles below.

1. When dogs and cats go out, what do they do? **Flip-Flop # _____**

2. What is a spot of paint that's no good? **Flip-Flop # _____**

3. Which fish-catching device is after nine? **Flip-Flop # _____**

4. Who is the physician for a kind of cold-water fish? **Flip-Flop # _____**

5. What kind of heavy cup holds your chewing sticks? **Flip-Flop # _____**

6. What is an underwater passenger vehicle? **Flip-Flop # _____**

7. Who have the biggest parts in the rodent show? **Flip-Flop # _____**

8. What is a quick, light touch? **Flip-Flop # _____**

9. What would you call a canine that people worship? **Flip-Flop # _____**

10. What are skin lumps on a scarecrow? **Flip-Flop # _____**

The Ultimate Homework Book © 2008 by Marvin Terban, Scholastic Teaching Resources

WHAT'S MISSING, PAL?

A whole sentence can be a palindrome. You can read it backward and forward and it is still the same sentence. (You just have to adjust the spaces sometimes.)

DIRECTIONS
Below you will find 10 palindrome sentences with words missing. Try to fill in the missing words. Remember, when the palindrome sentence is complete, you will be able to read it backward and forward. Hint: The underlined letters are the ones you have to flip to fill in the blanks.

1. <u>CIGAR? T</u>OSS IT IN A CAN, IT IS SO _____ .
   Clue: The person saying this hates cigars.

2. A TIN <u>MUG FOR</u> A JAR _____ , NITA.
   Clue: The person saying this loves to chew.

3. <u>MA HA</u>NDED EDNA _____ .
   Clue: It's something to eat.

4. <u>NAOMI</u> DID ____ _____ ?
   Clue: The person wants to know if he or she made a sound of pain.

5. NO _____ S. <u>NO MEL</u>ON.
   Clue: It's a yellow, oval citrus fruit.

6. NOW, _____ , A WA<u>R IS</u> WON.
   Clue: The person speaking is respectful.

7. <u>PAT</u> AND EDNA _____ .
   Clue: Pat and Edna are dancers.

8. _____ _____ IS I<u>N A DROOP</u>.
   Clue: This is about Daniel, who is sad.

9. <u>ROY, AM</u> I _____ ?
   Clue: The speaker wants to know if he or she has been elected head of the city.

10. <u>TOO</u> BAD I HID A _____ .
    Clue: What you hid is something you wear on your foot.

The Ultimate Homework Book © 2008 by Marvin Terban, Scholastic Teaching Resources

NOTHING TO FEAR!

A phobia is a fear. Everyone has phobias. That's natural. Sometimes it's a good thing because a fear can help keep us out of trouble. We want to avoid the things we're afraid of. Some fears are so common that they even have more than one phobia to name them.

You might guess that <u>comet</u>ophobia is the fear of getting hit by a comet, or that <u>dent</u>ophobia is the fear of going to a dentist. Figuring out the others will be more of a challenge because **phobia** is a Greek word, and the prefixes on the list of phobias below are Greek or Latin.

DIRECTIONS

Below are two columns of words: the names of phobias and what someone with those phobias would be afraid of. On the blank line in front of the phobia, put the letter of the fear. Use a dictionary or search engine, plus some clever thinking.

PHOBIAS	FEAR OF . . .
1. ____ **acarophobia** (also entomophobia)	**a.** bees
2. ____ **achluophobia**	**b.** being alone
3. ____ **acrophobia** (also altophobia)	**c.** darkness
4. ____ **algiophobia** (also aglophobia)	**d.** fire
5. ____ **agoraphobia**	**e.** flying
6. ____ **agrizoophobia**	**f.** heights
7. ____ **apiphobia**	**g.** insects, especially those that cause itching
8. ____ **arachnephobia** (also arachnophobia)	**h.** pain
9. ____ **arsonphobia**	**i.** pins, needles (sharp objects)
10. ____ **autophobia**	**j.** public spaces and crowds
11. ____ **aviatophobia** (also aerophobia and aviophobia)	**k.** spiders
12. ____ **belonephobia** (also aichmophobia)	**l.** wild animals

The Ultimate Homework Book © 2008 by Marvin Terban, Scholastic Teaching Resources

DON'T BE AFRAID!

A phobia is a fear. Everyone has phobias. That's natural. Sometimes it's a good thing because a fear can help keep us out of trouble. We want to avoid the things we're afraid of. Some fears are so common that they even have more than one phobia to name them.

You might guess that <u>insect</u>ophobia is the fear of insects, or that <u>snake</u>phobia is the fear of snakes. Figuring out the others will be more of a challenge because **phobia** is a Greek word, and the prefixes on the list of phobias below are Greek or Latin.

DIRECTIONS

Below are two columns of words: the names of phobias and what someone with those phobias would be afraid of. On the blank line in front of the phobia, put the letter of the fear. Use a dictionary or search engine, plus some clever thinking.

PHOBIAS	FEAR OF . . .
1. ____ **blennophobia**	**a.** blood
2. ____ **claustrophobia**	**b.** clowns
3. ____ **coulrophobia**	**c.** confined spaces
4. ____ **cynophobia**	**d.** dogs
5. ____ **glossophobia**	**e.** speaking in public
6. ____ **hemophobia** (also hematophobia)	**f.** doctors
7. ____ **helminthophobia**	**g.** horses
8. ____ **herpetophobia**	**h.** loud noises
9. ____ **hippophobia**	**i.** reptiles; creepy, crawly things
10. ____ **iatrophobia**	**j.** ridicule
11. ____ **katagelophobia**	**k.** worms
12. ____ **ligyrophobia**	**l.** slime

The Ultimate Homework Book © 2008 by Marvin Terban, Scholastic Teaching Resources

FEAR, DISAPPEAR!

A phobia is a fear. Everyone has phobias. That's natural. Sometimes it's a good thing because a fear can help keep us out of trouble. We want to avoid the things we're afraid of. Some fears are so common that they even have more than one phobia to name them.

You might guess that <u>bacterio</u>phobia is the fear of bacteria, or that <u>testo</u>phobia is the fear of taking tests. Figuring out the others will be more of a challenge because **phobia** is a Greek word, and the prefixes on the list of phobias below are Greek or Latin.

DIRECTIONS

Below are two columns of words: the names of phobias and what someone with those phobias would be afraid of. On the blank line in front of the phobia, put the letter of the fear. Use a dictionary or search engine, plus some clever thinking

PHOBIAS	FEAR OF . . .
1. ____ **lilapsophobia**	**a.** animals
2. ____ **logizomechanophobia**	**b.** ants
3. ____ **misophobia** (or mysophobia)	**c.** beards
4. ____ **musophobia** (or muriphobia)	**d.** being tickled by feathers
5. ____ **myrmecophobia**	**e.** computer
6. ____ **noctiphobia**	**f.** dirt
7. ____ **ophidiophobia**	**g.** ghosts
8. ____ **phasmophobia**	**h.** mice
9. ____ **pogonophobia**	**i.** night
10. ____ **pteronophobia**	**j.** snakes
11. ____ **triskaidekaphobia**	**k.** the number 13
12. ____ **zoophobia**	**l.** tornadoes and hurricanes

The Ultimate Homework Book © 2008 by Marvin Terban, Scholastic Teaching Resources

FIND THE PREPS

Only about 60 words in the English language are prepositions, but we couldn't write or speak without them. Prepositions tell us important facts, like where people and things are (location) and where they're going (direction). Here is a list of prepositions you hear, read, write, and say every day:

aboard	as	beyond	inside	over	toward
about	astride	but	into	past	under
above	at	by	like	regarding	underneath
across	before	despite	near	round	unlike
after	behind	down	of	since	until
against	below	during	off	than	up
along	beneath	except	on	through	upon
alongside	beside	for	onto	throughout	with
among	besides	from	out	till	within
around	between	in	outside	to	without

DIRECTIONS

In the story below, circle all the prepositions you can find. There is a total of 26. Use the list above as a guide. (One preposition is used three times.)

How to Get There

Mr. Blatt was standing on the corner of the street near his apartment house when a tall man with a wiggly beard asked him for directions to the nearest ATM machine. "Oh, that's easy," said Mr. Blatt. "It's very close. Just walk toward that tree with the purple leaves, go under the ornate overpass, and continue down the slippery hill to the raging waterfall. Proceed along the choppy river, behind the chicken restaurant, and stop at the candy store. Go between the gas station and the pickle factory, turn left, run through the scary tunnel and around the smelly swamp. After a few minutes, you will see a statue of a turnip near a garden of green feathers. Go up the humongous mountain, and past the fearsome forest. The ATM machine is outside the Cave of the Incredible Creatures."

"Forget it," said the man with the wiggly beard.

The Ultimate Homework Book © 2008 by Marvin Terban, Scholastic Teaching Resources

PHRASE CRAZE

A prepositional phrase is a group of words that starts with a preposition and ends with one or more words called the "object of the preposition."

Prepositional phrases are usually two, three, or four words long, but they can be longer. For example, "Over the river and through the woods to grandmother's house we go" has three prepositional phrases: **over the river**, **through the woods**, and **to grandmother's house**.

DIRECTIONS

In the sentences below, circle all the prepositions. There is just one in every sentence. Then underline all the prepositional phrases. Then draw a box around the object of the preposition at the end of each prepositional phrase. It should look like this:

> **TiP**
> All the prepositions in these sentences begin with the same letter.

The butterfly landed ⊙on the buffalo's ☐nose☐.

1. When I got aboard the ship, I was happy sailing the seven seas, plus some oceans, rivers, lakes, creeks, streams, and ponds.

2. When she told me about her adventures, I could hardly stop laughing.

3. Above our heads flew a weirdly decorated alien space vehicle.

4. I dashed across the street and told my cousin the hilarious story.

5. The champion squash player kept hitting the ball against the wall.

6. After an hour, I took my pretzels and left the aquarium.

7. I could see the little snake slithering silently alongside the roadside.

8. I never understood why he was so popular among the neighborhood cats.

9. We just took a leisurely walk around the jungle and heard many adorable tigers, lions, leopards, gorillas, zebras, and elephants growling, howling, bellowing, roaring, and trumpeting.

10. He looked at the king's magnificent palace and said, "Nice place, king."

The Ultimate Homework Book © 2008 by Marvin Terban, Scholastic Teaching Resources

PHRASE MAZE

Prepositional phrases tell four things:

   1. LOCATION (where):

     Your new orange sweater is hanging **in the hallway closet**.

   2. DIRECTION (where to or where from):

     He ran quickly **into the ice cream shop**.

   3. TIME (when):

     I'll help you with your "Dinosaurs Are Birds" science project **after lunch**.

If a prepositional phrase doesn't show location, direction, or time, then it's showing:

   4. RELATIONSHIP BETWEEN WORDS:

     The story was written **by Lord Hoarsly Croaker**.

     (In this sentence, the preposition **by** shows the relationship between the story and its author: the story was written by Lord Croaker.)

DIRECTIONS

In the sentences below, the prepositional phrases are already underlined for you. Over each phrase print a capital **L**, **D**, **T**, or **R** to show if the phrase is indicating Location, Direction, Time, or Relationship.

1. I was so hungry, I ate my lunch <u>before school</u>.

2. Meet me <u>by the pumpkin patch</u> and I'll tell you the gerbil's name.

3. The mighty eagle flew <u>beyond the blue horizon</u>.

4. The bee stung the teacher's nose <u>during history class</u>.

5. An onion came flying <u>from the tower window</u>.

6. The King <u>of Pedsylvania</u> always wore one blue shoe and one red shoe.

7. <u>Since Thursday</u> the drumming hasn't stopped, and it's driving me crazy!

8. <u>Throughout his lifetime</u> my grandfather's square oranges were loved.

9. I can help you wallpaper the horse's stable <u>until snack time</u>.

10. George went <u>with Loraine</u> to find the secret map.

The Ultimate Homework Book © 2008 by Marvin Terban, Scholastic Teaching Resources

YOU AND I AND OTHER PRONOUNS

A pronoun is a word that takes the place of a noun.

Use a subject pronoun for the subject of a verb.

The subject is the word that names the person, place, thing, or idea that the sentence is mainly about. The subject performs the action of the verb.

Here are the subject pronouns:

I   you   he   she   it   we   they

DIRECTIONS

In the sentences below, circle all the subject pronouns. Be careful. There are other kinds of pronouns mixed in. Just circle the ones used as subjects.

1. "I don't want to give her a lick of my lollipop," he shouted.

2. After the concert, they went back to their house for ice cream.

3. Once she was a princess, but now she gives haircuts to dogs.

4. We must remember to take the hamster with us on vacation or it will be lonely.

5. You must never forget that we rescued your duck from the stuck roller coaster.

6. I knew they wouldn't like it if we ate all their popcorn during the movie.

7. He and she used to speak Wu when they were little, but they forgot it.

8. It can't be true that you and she saw them wearing chicken costumes.

9. He's so tall that his mother has to stand on a ladder to kiss him.

10. Right now I'm so tired I could sleep for a week at his house.

The Ultimate Homework Book © 2008 by Marvin Terban, Scholastic Teaching Resources

HIM AND ME AND OTHER PRONOUNS

Use an object pronoun for the three kinds of objects in a sentence:

- direct object
- indirect object
- object of a preposition

Here are all seven object pronouns:

me   you   him   her

it   us   them

DIRECTIONS

In the sentences below, circle all the object pronouns. There are other kinds of pronouns mixed in, so be careful. Be especially careful about **you** and **it**. Sometimes they're subjects. Sometimes they're objects. Circle only the pronouns used as direct objects, indirect objects, or objects of prepositions. Hint: There could be more than one object pronoun in a sentence, and some are used more than once.

TIP

You and **it** lead double lives. They can be used as both subjects and objects!

1. When she saw him dressed as a frog, she screamed, "Gribbit! Gribbit!"

2. They want us to go to the principal's office immediately.

3. Please call them and say that you can't dance the cha-cha-cha tonight.

4. If I told you once, I told you a million times, don't whistle while eating peanut butter.

5. She gave me the money, I put it in my sock, and I lost it in the dryer.

6. It broke down on the road and stranded us near Albuquerque.

7. She beat him in the swim meet, but he beat her in the cooking contest.

8. You know that I want you to sing in the show, but they want him.

9. When you gave it to him, did he at least say, "Thank you"?

10. Serve her the cake, him the pie, them the cookies, and us the muffins.

The Ultimate Homework Book © 2008 by Marvin Terban, Scholastic Teaching Resources

YOURS AND MINE AND OTHER PRONOUNS

Use a possessive pronoun to show possession (ownership).

There are 12 possessive pronouns:

my	mine
your	yours
his	
her	hers
its	
our	ours
their	theirs

TIP
A possessive pronoun never has an apostrophe.

DIRECTIONS

In the sentences below, circle all the possessive pronouns. Be careful. This is tricky. Subject and object pronouns are mixed in. Don't circle them.

1. Her dog tap dances while his hamster plays the piano. It's a cute act!

2. The directions say that theirs is the third house on the right.

3. I know that my mother won't let us do it, but let's ask anyway.

4. The truck lost its wheel going around the bend, and now it's stuck in the mud.

5. That's mine, not yours, so give it back!

6. They're painting their house with purple polka dots right over there.

7. Hers is a tale of bravery, heroism, and lollipops.

8. You're not going to take your toys and go home now, are you?

9. Her grandmother gave her a pet hippo for her birthday.

10. I'm ready to cook his recipe in their pots for our dinner.

The Ultimate Homework Book © 2008 by Marvin Terban, Scholastic Teaching Resources

BE A PRONOUN DETECTIVE

A pronoun is a word that takes the place of a noun. The subject, object, and possessive pronouns are as follows:

I	you	he	she	it	we	they	my
mine	your	yours	his	her	hers	its	our
ours	their	theirs	me	him	us	them	

DIRECTIONS

In the story below, circle all the pronouns you can find from the list of 23 pronouns above.

HINT #1
You have to circle 36 pronouns in this story. Some are used more than once.

HINT #2
Watch out for contractions that begin with pronouns. Just circle the pronouns at the beginning, not the rest of the word.

A Book for a Bat

Loraine and George had been friends since first grade. She was one month older than he was, but he was four inches taller than she was. They lived across the street from a beautiful park. "This park is ours," she once said. She liked to go to the park to read. He liked to go there to play ball. Then one day, she said to him, "I have a good idea for us. If you let me borrow your bat, I will let you read my favorite book."

"It's a deal," he said. "We have lots of books at our house, but I've read them all."

"And I don't have a baseball bat at my house, so that's why I have to borrow yours."

Their idea was a good one, and they had a perfect day. Hers was a good book, and she played ball with his bat. They were quite happy with the switch they had made.

The Ultimate Homework Book © 2008 by Marvin Terban, Scholastic Teaching Resources

FILL IN THE MISSING PRONOUNS

A pronoun is a word that takes the place of a noun. The subject, object, and possessive pronouns are as follows:

I	you	he	she	it	we	they	my
mine	your	yours	his	her	hers	its	our
ours	their	theirs	me	him	us	them	

DIRECTIONS

From the list of pronouns above, fill in the blanks in the sentences below. The clues in parentheses will help you decide which pronouns to write in.

1. _____ (belongs to me) puppy ate all _____ (belongs to it) dinner.

2. Please tell _____ (the girl) to take _____ (belongs to me) tuba.

3. I saw _____ (those people) paint _____ (the thing) with orange stripes.

4. This pecan pie is _____ (belongs to us), not _____ (belongs to them).

5. _____ (the boy) shouted to _____ (the girl), "_____ (the thing) won't run until you charge _____ (belongs to it) batteries."

6. _____ (the person speaking) love _____ (the thing) when a rainbow comes out after a rainstorm.

7. _____ (the man) thought that _____ (the woman) had paid too much money for _____ (the object), but _____ (the woman) liked _____ (the object) so much, _____ (the woman) kept _____ (the object).

8. _____ (belongs to us) school is having _____ (belongs to it) annual holiday dance at _____ (belongs to me) uncle's restaurant.

9. If _____ (the person spoken to) ever show _____ (the thing) to _____ (those people), _____ (the person speaking) will never speak to _____ (the person spoken to) again!

10. _____ (belongs to her) brother saw _____ (belongs to you) sister walking with _____ (the boy) in the park.

The Ultimate Homework Book © 2008 by Marvin Terban, Scholastic Teaching Resources

YOU REALLY NEED PRONOUNS!

A pronoun is a word that takes the place of a noun. The pronouns are as follows:

I	you	he	she	it	we	they	my
mine	your	yours	his	her	hers	its	our
ours	their	theirs	me	him	us	them	

DIRECTIONS
To prove how much pronouns help to make English easier to use, cross out any unnecessary words in the story below and replace them with the appropriate pronouns from the list above.

TiP
You can put in as many as 38 pronouns.

Jen and Tim

It was Jen's first day of school. Jen jumped out of Jen's bed and took a fast shower. Jen then looked in Jen's mirror and said to Jenself, "Jen looks great today." Then Jen ate Jen's breakfast, picked up Jen's backpack, kissed Jen's mother and father, and waved goodbye to Jen's mother and father as Jen flew out the door.

On the way to Jen's school, Jen met Jen's next-door neighbor, Tim. "Hi, Tim," Jen called to Tim. "Can Jen and Tim walk to school together?"

"Sure," Tim said. Then Tim asked, "Would Jen like Tim to carry Jen's backpack?"

Jen answered, "No, thanks. Jen can do it Jenself."

And off Jen and Tim went, carrying Jen's and Tim's own backpacks to school.

"Lucky Jen and Tim," Tim said.

"Why are Jen and Tim so lucky?" Jen asked.

"Because Jen and Tim go to such a great school. Jen and Tim have great teachers. And even the food in Jen and Tim's cafeteria is great."

"Tim's right," Jen said. "Jen and Tim are lucky."

The Ultimate Homework Book © 2008 by Marvin Terban, Scholastic Teaching Resources

WHAT'S AT THE END?

Every sentence has a punctuation mark at the end.

PERIOD	comes at the end of all regular sentences that just make statements
QUESTION MARK	comes at the end of any sentence that asks a question
EXCLAMATION POINT (sometimes called an exclamation mark)	comes at the end of a sentence that expresses strong feelings or emotions

DIRECTIONS

Put either a period, a question mark, or an exclamation point at the end of each sentence below. Sometimes a sentence can have either a period or an exclamation mark at the end, depending on how intense the sentence is.

1. My name is Baron Egbert von Loopingdorf Schnitzelheim III

2. The volcano has erupted, and hot, molten lava is rushing down the mountainside toward our village

3. I saw the biggest movie star in the world at the mall

4. Math class is next

5. At what temperature does water freeze

6. There's no school today because of the snowstorm

7. Many people think that the biggest tree in the world is in Santa Maria del Tule, a small town in the state of Oaxaca, Mexico

8. I hate peanut butter and broccoli sandwiches

9. Are you the boy who rescued the gerbils from the cat

10. The giant model of Tyrannosaurus rex has come alive

11. Is the Statue of Liberty in New York or New Jersey

12. Run for the hills

The Ultimate Homework Book © 2008 by Marvin Terban, Scholastic Teaching Resources

FAMOUS QUOTES QUOTED

When you write down someone's exact words, you are quoting him or her directly.

There are three main parts to punctuating direct quotations:

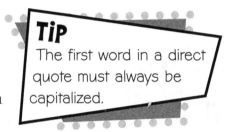

1. The exact words someone said

2. The person who said them

3. A verb like **said**, **asked**, **shouted**, etc.

This is how you punctuate direct quotes when the person speaking comes first:

Mr. X said, "Blah blah blah blah blah."

Mr. X asked, "Blah blah blah blah blah?"

Mr. X screamed, "Blah blah blah blah blah!"

DIRECTIONS

The sentences below contain direct quotes from some well-known people. Add four punctuation marks to each sentence to make it complete.

> **TiP**
> The first word in a direct quote must always be capitalized.

1. In 1897, 13 years before he died, Mark Twain pronounced   The report of my death was an exaggeration

2. One of the best American singers ever, Marian Anderson, wisely said   Everyone has a gift for something, even if it is the gift of being a good friend

3. Charles Dickens must have read a lot of bad books because he once stated   There are books of which the backs and covers are by far the best parts

4. Ben Franklin, who accomplished a lot in his life, gave pretty good advice when he said   Early to bed and early to rise, makes a man healthy, wealthy, and wise

5. Albert Einstein must have known what he was talking about when he suggested   Anyone who has never made a mistake has never tried anything new

6. Although she was definitely a somebody, it's strange that the great American poet of the 1800s, Emily Dickinson, once asked   I'm nobody! Who are you

7. Thomas Jefferson uttered something worth thinking about when he observed   I find that the harder I work, the more luck I seem to have

8. Singer, actress, writer, and activist Maya Angelou once declared   How important it is for us to recognize and celebrate our heroes and she-roes

The Ultimate Homework Book © 2008 by Marvin Terban, Scholastic Teaching Resources

GET ON THE QUOTE BOAT!

When you write down someone's exact words, you are quoting him or her directly.

There are three main parts to punctuating direct quotations:

1. The exact words someone said
2. The person who said them
3. A verb like **said**, **asked**, **shouted**, etc.

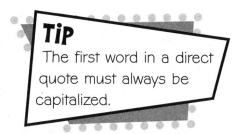

TiP
The first word in a direct quote must always be capitalized.

This is how you punctuate direct quotes when the quote comes first:

"Blah blah blah blah blah?" **asked Mr. X.**

"Blah blah blah blah blah," **said Mr. X.**

"Blah blah blah blah blah!" **howled Mr. X.**

"Bon appetit!"

DIRECTIONS
Add four missing punctuation marks to each sentence below to make it complete.

1. What ingredients did you put in this fabulous stew   Alberto asked the new chef

2. Four score and seven years ago   said Abraham Lincoln at the beginning of his Gettysburg Address

3. Make sure the baby is in bed by eight o'clock   Mrs. Youngman instructed the babysitter

4. Class, today's big test has been cancelled because of a shortage of sharpened pencils   stated the professor with a sigh

5. Don't bite down   screamed the hysterical dentist with his finger still in the patient's mouth

6. Which river carries the greatest volume of water, the Amazon or the Nile   asked the geography teacher

7. Who did this   wondered my aunt in her soft, but quizzical, voice

8. The Statue of Liberty was brought across the Atlantic Ocean by ship from France in 350 pieces in 1885 stated the brochure.

The Ultimate Homework Book © 2008 by Marvin Terban, Scholastic Teaching Resources

WHO BROKE THESE QUOTES?

When you write down someone's exact words, you are quoting him or her directly.

There are three main parts to punctuating direct quotations:

1. The exact words someone said

2. The person who said them

3. A verb like **said**, **asked**, **shouted**, etc.

Sometimes the direct quotation is broken into two pieces. The person speaking comes in the middle, like this:

"Blah blah blah," **said Mrs. X,** "blah blah."

"Blah blah blah," **asked Mrs. X,** "blah blah?"

"Blah blah blah," **yelled Mrs. X,** "blah blah!"

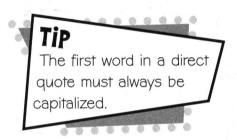

DIRECTIONS

All of the sentences below have broken quotes. Add seven punctuation marks to each sentence to make it complete.

TiP

The first word in a direct quote must always be capitalized.

1. I never wear orange hats said the movie star   because orange doesn't go well with my hazel eyes

2. When you add salt to this soup instructed the cooking teacher   just a pinch will do

3. Thanks for getting me that DVD for my birthday said his grandson   because science-fiction horror movies are my favorites

4. You're playing left field today called the coach and make sure you keep your head up during the game

5. How can you study for your history test   asked her mother   with the music turned up so high

6. Hurry and turn on the TV   shouted my aunt   as she ran into the room because Uncle Harry's being interviewed on the news

7. I used to know the names of all the highest mountains   said my friend   but I can't remember them now

8. Are you going to the same camp this summer   asked the girl behind me in line or a new one

The Ultimate Homework Book © 2008 by Marvin Terban, Scholastic Teaching Resources

WHAT DID YOU SAY?

When you write down someone's exact words, you are quoting him or her directly.

There are three main parts to punctuating direct quotations:

1. The exact words someone said

2. The person who said them

3. A verb like **said**, **asked**, **shouted**, etc.

Remember, the first word in a direct quote must always be capitalized.

Mr. X said, "Blah blah blah blah blah."

"Blah blah blah blah blah?" asked Mr. X.

"Blah blah blah blah blah," shouted Mr. X, "blah blah blah!"

TiP
The number in parentheses at the end of each sentence tells you how many punctuation marks you have to add.

DIRECTIONS
Add in the missing punctuation to complete the sentences below.

1. The teacher asked Does anyone know if Jászalsószentgyörgy is in Poland or Hungary (4)

2. The Tyrannosaurus rex is loose cried the zookeeper (4)

3. I know what the secret of Goo La La is she whispered softly but I'm never going to reveal it (7)

4. The big sign at the front door stated simply Step into the haunted house on your right foot first (4)

5. President William Howard Taft kept a cow on the White House lawn the famous historian said and she slept in the garage (7)

6. She whispered A tomato is really a fruit and ran into the bushes (5)

7. Why did you wear your pants on your head asked his mother (4)

8. My neighbor yelled from across the street Turn down that music because the noise is driving me crazy (4)

9. My name is Loraine she explained but I spell it with only one *r* in the middle (7)

10. I won the election at last exclaimed the jubilant candidate (4)

The Ultimate Homework Book © 2008 by Marvin Terban, Scholastic Teaching Resources

COMMA SENSE

Commas are very useful punctuation marks, but people often put them in the wrong places or don't put them in at all!

DIRECTIONS

In the following sentences, put commas between words so the reader will pause and not be confused. Also, put commas between items in a list.

1. To Jennifer Timothy was the best singer in the world.

2. After the broken roller coaster shut down down came the repairmen from the top level.

3. At the supermarket I bought peanut butter apple pie ice cream and corn flakes.

4. The king walked in in his royal robes.

5. For my pets I always have a supply of kitty litter chewy bones flea spray and bird seed.

6. When the monsters came out out ran the frightened kid.

7. In the costume department you'll find suits of armor witches' hats soldiers' uniforms and wedding gowns.

8. The dancer twirled on on her new dancing shoes.

9. At my drug store I sell baby powder razor blades hair brushes and electric toothbrushes.

10. When the rocket shot up up went all our eyes to follow it.

The Ultimate Homework Book © 2008 by Marvin Terban, Scholastic Teaching Resources

COMMA-RAMA

Commas are very useful punctuation marks,
but people often put them in the wrong places
or don't put them in at all!

DIRECTIONS
In the following sentences, put commas
between words so the reader will pause and not
be confused. Also, put commas between items
in a list.

1. For the picnic she packed a blanket bug spray cheese sandwiches plastic cups and iced tea.

2. For Mrs. Thomas Richard will be the best person to cut her hair.

3. As the dark storm clouds gathered above above our heads we heard the sound of thunder.

4. A few minutes after the thunderstorm came.

5. Before the crowd drew near near the speaker a microphone was placed.

6. For Halloween I wore a mask fashioned from colored paper and chicken feathers a blouse created from an old pillowcase a skirt made from neckties and boots that were really big plastic bottles.

7. Even though her best friend is Mary Jane voted for Susie in the election.

8. After the plane flew over over at the airport the people cheered.

9. Just the day before the Broadway show opened.

10. At college my brother studies American history French literature Egyptian hieroglyphics and Chinese cooking.

The Ultimate Homework Book © 2008 by Marvin Terban, Scholastic Teaching Resources

POEMS ABOUT YOUR FRIENDS

Rhymes are words that sound alike at their ends, like **spin**, **within**, and **violin**. The parts that rhyme don't have to be spelled alike. Just look at **buy**, **cry**, **high**, **rye**, and **tie**. Poems don't have to rhyme, but many people like them when they do.

DIRECTIONS
From the group of words below, choose words that fit onto the blank lines in the poems that follow, and make them rhyme. The first one is started for you. Note: **Chuck** and **ghost** are used twice.

note	boat	Chuck	clothes	float	coat	down	duck	frown
ghost	glue	gnu	goat	goes	gown	host	Lou	luck
most	nose	blows	roast	Rose	shoe	boast	stuck	~~clown~~
toast	toes	town	truck	true	wrote	zoo		

1. My friend the _clown_

   Put on her _____ ,

   And then went walking into _____ ,

   But, oops!, she slipped and fell

   right _____

   And now she wears a forlorn _____ .

2. My friend the _____

   _____ me a _____

   To sail away on his big _____ ;

   So I put on my rubber _____

   And off I went to sail and _____ .

3. My friend named _____

   Who works at the _____

   Got _____ on his _____

   And it stuck to the _____ ;

   It's _____ !

4. My friend named _____

   Was driving his _____ ,

   But it got _____

   Behind a slow _____ ;

   Bad _____ , _____ !

5. My friend _____

   _____ her _____ ,

   Polishes her _____ ,

   Puts on her _____ ,

   And out she _____ .

6. My friend the _____

   Is a perfect _____ ;

   He cooks a tasty pot of _____ ,

   And serves it up with butter and

   _____ ;

   I really do not like to _____ ,

   But you must admit my _____'s

   the _____ !

The Ultimate Homework Book © 2008 by Marvin Terban, Scholastic Teaching Resources

FILL IN THE MISSING RHYMES

Sometimes every other line of a poem rhymes, like this:

> While walking down the street one **day**;
>
> I saw the strangest <u>sight</u>:
>
> A dancing dog on a bale of **hay**;
>
> Now how could that be <u>right</u>?

DIRECTIONS

Choose two pairs of rhyming words from the group of words below to write on the blank lines in the poems that follow. The first line should rhyme with the third line. The second line should rhyme with the fourth line. Make sure the poems make sense after you fill in the blanks.

head	breaks	ball	grooming	bitter	mow
red	cakes	wall	blooming	critter	grow
mop	cheering	tasty	freezing	white	bowl
shop	hearing	pasty	sneezing	height	soul

1. Winter days are awfully _____ ,
   The temperature is _____ ;
   And every little chilly _____
   Is shivering and _____ .

2. The soft thin hair atop his

   _____
   Has turned three shades of

   _____ ;
   But once his hair was thick

   and _____ ,
   And awesome in its _____ .

3. I swing the bat and hit the

   _____ ,
   The crowd is up and _____ ;
   The ball flies way beyond the

   _____ ;
   I love the cheers I'm _____ .

4. The chicken noodles in my

   _____
   Are slippery and _____ ;
   They thaw my bones and warm

   my _____ ,
   And make my face less

   _____ .

5. She loves to sweep, she loves

   to _____ ,
   She takes no cleaning _____ ;
   She loves to scrub her pastry

   _____ ;
   She even dusts the _____ !

6. His lawn he loves to _____ ,
   His yard he's always _____ ,
   He sees his flowers _____ ,
   He sees his garden _____ .

The Ultimate Homework Book © 2008 by Marvin Terban, Scholastic Teaching Resources

YOU'RE A POET AND DON'T KNOW IT

DIRECTIONS

Now it's time for you to try your hand at being a poet. Below are four groups of rhyming words. Choose words from one group and make up a four-line poem that has the same rhyming sound at the end of every line. It's a good idea to use scrap paper when you try to write a poem because you'll probably change a lot of words around until you get the poem the way you want it. When you've got your poem the way you want it, copy it neatly onto the four blank lines below.

TIP
Make each line rhyme with the same rhyming sound.

be, bee, fee, flea, flee, free, gee, glee, he, key, me, pea, plea, sea, see, she, ski, spree, tea, three, tree, we, wee

cool, cruel, drool, fool, fuel, mule, pool, rule, school, spool, stool, tool, who'll, you'll, yule

boar, bore, chore, core, corps, door, floor, for, four, lore, more, oar, or, ore, pore, pour, roar, score, shore, snore, soar, sore, store, swore, tore, war, wore, your

blaze, days, daze, gaze, glaze, graze, haze, maze, pays, phase, phrase, plays, praise, prays, preys, raise, rays, slays, sleighs, sprays, stays, strays, sways, weighs

_____

_____

_____

_____

The Ultimate Homework Book © 2008 by Marvin Terban, Scholastic Teaching Resources

IT'S TIME TO RHYME

DIRECTIONS

Below are six groups of rhyming words. Choose words from two groups and make up a four-line poem in which every other line rhymes. You might want to compose your poems on scrap paper first because poetry writing takes a lot of crossing out and changing. Then make a neat copy of your poem on the blank lines below. Make sure your poem make sense when you're finished.

TiP

Make the first and third lines rhyme. Make the second and fourth lines rhyme.

bing, bring, cling, ding, fling, king, ping, ring, sing, spring, sting, string, swing, ting, wing, wring, zing

beat, beet, bleat, cheat, eat, feat, feet, fleet, greet, heat, meat, meet, neat, seat, sheet, sleet, street, suite, sweet, treat, wheat

beak, cheek, creak, creek, freak, leak, leek, meek, peak, peek, seek, sheik, shriek, sleek, sneak, speak, squeak, streak, tweak, weak, week

blew, blue, boo, crew, chew, clue, coo, crew, cue, dew, do, drew, due, few, flew, flu, flue, glue, goo, grew, knew, moo, new, shoe, strew, threw, through, to, too, true, two, view, who, woo, you, zoo

blocks, box, clocks, docks, flocks, fox, frocks, knocks, locks, lox, mocks, ox, pox, rocks, shocks, smocks, socks, sox, stocks

buy, by, bye, cry, die, dry, dye, eye, fly, fry, guy, hi, high, I, lie, lye, my, pie, pry, rye, shy, sigh, sky, sly, spry, spy, sty, thigh, tie, try, why, wry

_____

_____

_____

_____

The Ultimate Homework Book © © 2008 by Marvin Terban, Scholastic Teaching Resources

ADD -ES OR -S? WHAT TO DO?

A noun is a word that names a person, place, thing, or idea. Most nouns just add **-s** when they go from singular (just one) to plural (more than one).

SINGULAR NOUNS	PLURAL NOUNS
pencil	pencils
sister	sisters
football	footballs

If a singular noun ends with **-s**, **-ss**, **-ch**, **-sh**, or **-x**, add **-es** (not **-s**) to make it plural.

SINGULAR NOUNS	PLURAL NOUNS
address	addresses
pitch	pitches
fox	foxes

DIRECTIONS

In the following sentences, make every singular noun in boldface plural. Add **-s** to some words and **-es** to others.

1. I told my little brother never to play with **match**____ .

2. The two white **tiger**____ at the zoo were cool.

3. That baby has the longest **eyelash**____ I've ever seen.

4. Four **class**____ are going on the school trip today.

5. Our team won three **medal**____ in the writing contest.

6. During the protest **march**____ we will carry **torch**____ .

7. Please help me carry these **box**____ up the stairs.

8. The café serves the biggest **breakfast**____ in town.

9. I looked in four **atlas**____ , but I still can't find Andorra.

10. After he broke his ankle, he walked with **crutch**____ .

The Ultimate Homework Book © 2008 by Marvin Terban, Scholastic Teaching Resources

ADD -S OR -ES?
THAT IS THE QUESTION!

A **noun** is a word that names a person, place, thing, or idea. Most nouns **just add s** when they go from singular (just one) to plural (more than one).

SINGULAR NOUNS	PLURAL NOUNS
jellybean	jellybeans
toenail	toenails
elephant	elephants

If a singular noun ends with **-s**, **-ss**, **-ch**, **-sh**, or **-x**, add **-es** (not **-s**) to make it plural.

SINGULAR NOUNS	PLURAL NOUNS
albatross	albatrosses
arch	arches
cineplex	cineplexes

DIRECTIONS

In the following sentences, make every singular noun in boldface plural.
Add **-s** to some words and **-es** to others.

1. Every April 15, my parents pay their **tax___** .

2. A lot of kids dress up as **witch___** on Halloween.

3. The new **computer___** in my classroom are awesome!

4. Hikers, do your **compass___** show we're going west?

5. There are no major **metropolis___** in this tiny country.

6. Did you see those **flash___** of light in the sky?

7. My English teacher taught us many Latin **prefix___** .

8. Look at all the **scratch___** I got from that kitten.

9. They sell fancy dog **leash___** in this pet store.

10. The **skyscraper___** in New York are huge.

The Ultimate Homework Book © 2008 by Marvin Terban, Scholastic Teaching Resources

Y? Y NOT?

Many nouns in English end with the letter **y**. When you want to make one of these nouns plural, look at the letter in front of the y. If that letter is a vowel (a, e, i, o, u), just add **-s**. The noun is now plural. For example:

That **boy** and two other **boys** danced the hula.

When the letter in front of the final **y** is a consonant (any letter that's not a vowel) change the **y** to **i** and add **-es**. For example:

That **lady** and two other **ladies** changed the tire.

DIRECTIONS

In the sentences below, some nouns are in boldface. Above each of these words, print the plural of that word. Make sure to look at the letter in front of the final **y** to decide what to do.

1. All the **birthday** in my family are in August.

2. My brother went to six **country** on his vacation.

3. Those aren't real ducks; they're just **decoy**.

4. My dentist said I didn't have any **cavity** this time.

5. My grandmother's house has tall **chimney**.

6. I went to three travel **agency** to get my tickets.

7. We chased the runaway dog through narrow **alley**.

8. I always put **blueberry** in my cereal.

9. You can get some really good **buy** at this mall.

10. You need two AA **battery** for this camera.

The Ultimate Homework Book © 2008 by Marvin Terban, Scholastic Teaching Resources

ODD PLURALS!

Sometimes nouns change to plurals in unpredictable ways. You may have to change the spelling of a singular noun to make it plural.
For example:

I **man** + I **man** = 2 **men**.

Or, you may not have to change the spelling at all.

DIRECTIONS
In each sentence below you'll find one singular noun in boldface. Above each singular noun, print its plural spelling. If you're not sure, the dictionary will help you.

1. Mrs. Youngman took five **child** to the circus.

2. A flock of honking **goose** woke me up last night.

3. I think some **mouse** have been nibbling the cheese.

4. Those two **ox** look very big, don't they?

5. My little sister lost two **tooth** in one week.

6. Hurry up! Pick up your **foot** or we'll be late.

7. Four **woman** are waiting to see you, doctor.

8. Please help me put these books on those **shelf.**

9. Did you see those three **deer** run by the window?

10. Graduates from a school are called **alumnus.**

★ ★ ★ ★ ★ ★ ★ ★

Challenge

Find another example of a noun that names an animal and is spelled the same way in both its singular and plural forms.

The Ultimate Homework Book © 2008 by Marvin Terban, Scholastic Teaching Resources

RULE BREAKERS

There's a famous spelling rule in the form
of a poem that goes like this:

I before **E**

Except after **C**

Or when sounding like **A**

As in **neighbor** or **weigh**

That rule/poem works for a lot of words, like **believe**
("i before e"), **ceiling** ("except after c"), and **eight** ("or when sounding
like a"). But it doesn't work for many other words. These rule-breaker
words are spelled "e before i"—or "i before e," **after** c.

DIRECTIONS

In each sentence below, there are two words that break the "i before e" rule in the
poem above. Find them and circle them. (Be careful: There are words that follow the
rule in some of the sentences, too. Don't circle them.)

1. In ancient times there were different species of animals than we have today.

2. The scientists invented some weird stuff.

3. The foreign sleigh was pulled by either reindeer or frogs.

4. Did the heir to the kingdom have sufficient leisure time during his brief reign?

5. "Don't eat too much pie or you'll gain weight," said the seismologist to
   the financier.

6. They had to forfeit their game because two players didn't show up.

7. "Caffeine isn't too good for you, but protein is," said the chief.

8. Being eight is a good age, but I wish my height was higher.

9. The thief seized the golden kaleidoscope and ran out the door.

10. "This society worked very efficiently for more than eight hundred years," lectured
    the professor.

The Ultimate Homework Book © 2008 by Marvin Terban, Scholastic Teaching Resources

PUT BACK THE MISSING LETTERS!

Some words in English have weird beginnings. They start with a letter you don't pronounce. You ignore the sound of the first letter and start with the sound of the second letter. For example, a **gnat** is a little fly that's like a mosquito. But you pronounce the name of these annoying insects "nats" not "g-nats." The **g** is silent. Other words like this begin with **kn-**, **ps-**, **pt-**, **pn-**, and **wr-**.

DIRECTIONS

In the following sentences there are words that are spelled wrong on purpose. The first letter of each of these words—the letter you don't pronounce—has been left out. Find these words and write the first letters back in. Insert the letter like this:

k

She had a ⌃nack for saying just the right thing.

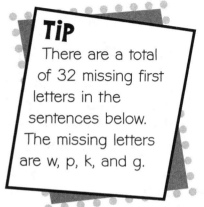

TiP
There are a total of 32 missing first letters in the sentences below. The missing letters are w, p, k, and g.

1. In the car reck the sychologist broke his rist, his nee and one of his nuckles.

2. At the zoo, the new nu nawed through the yew tree.

3. The retched sychiatrist got tomaine poisoning from eating the rong foods and neumonia from some bacteria.

4. The forest nome was guarding the magical, golden nob that the night had buried.

5. If you carefully rap the sick ren so it doesn't riggle too much and nock on the veterinarian's door, you will save its life.

6. Don't restle with your brother in your new shirt or you'll rinkle it.

7. The sychic new I had a nife in my napsack.

8. The baker rote out the proper way to nead the dough.

9. My grandma nitted her pet terodactyl an adorable sweater.

10. Please don't nash your teeth when I tell you to make a double not in your shoelaces and to ring out your bathing suit.

The Ultimate Homework Book © 2008 by Marvin Terban, Scholastic Teaching Resources

SHHH! FIND THE SILENT LETTERS!

Several letters can be silent when they are inside or at the end of words.
For example:

> doubt, hedge, align, ghetto, salmon, solemn, receipt, mortgage, and guess

Even though you don't pronounce these letters when you say the words aloud, you must put them in when you spell the words.

DIRECTIONS
In the following sentences, find the words that have silent letters inside or at the ends. (Double letters don't count.) Circle those silent letters like this:

TIP
At the end, you should have circled 48 silent letters.

Last autumn, I ate a lot of almonds.

1. The plumber who lived in Connecticut climbed the ladder.

2. Last Wednesday, the handsome man lost his handkerchief.

3. Thomas rhymed "ghost" with "most" and "post."

4. Abraham Lincoln sang a solemn hymn in Illinois at Christmas.

5. The raspberry in the cupboard came from an island in Arkansas.

6. Listen to the guard with the badge at the castle talk to the folk.

7. The sign was on the column in the building on the aisle.

8. Eat your biscuit, play your guitar, fasten the latch, and answer the door.

9. The butcher sighed when the guilty guest ate half the yolk.

10. Where did you see the calm calf, the lamb in the isle, the palm tree, and the debris?

The Ultimate Homework Book © 2008 by Marvin Terban, Scholastic Teaching Resources

WHAT LETTER SHOULD I PUT IN?

Spelling the ends of some words can be really confusing because they are so much alike. For example, some words end with **-able** and some with **-ible** (valuable and responsible). Some end with **-tion** and some with **-sion** (constellation and collision). Some end with **-er** and some with **-or** (leader and decorator). Some end with **-ious** and some with **-eous** (hilarious and hideous). That's really confusing!

DIRECTIONS

In the sentences below, a letter has been left out of the words in boldface. Fill in that missing letter. If in doubt, consult your friendly dictionary.

1. The teacher knows I am **cap__ble** of doing **accept__ble** work, but my last paper was **illeg__ble**, and it will not be **poss__ble** to get an A on it.

2. The **courag__ous** hero fought off the **feroc__ous** monster.

3. My **sist__r** is very talented. She's a **danc__r**, a **sing__r**, and an **act__r**.

4. **Atten__ion**, everyone! After the **elec__ion** results are announced, there will be an **explo__ion** of fireworks as part of the **celebra__ion**.

5. That movie was **terr__ble**, **horr__ble**, and **deplor__ble**, and it's **unbeliev__ble** and **inexcus__ble** that you paid good money to see it!

6. It's the story of a **hid__ous** monster, a **gorg__ous** princess, a **fur__ous** king, a **myster__ous** wizard, a **malic__ous** villain, and a **court__ous** prince.

7. The **may__r**, the **govern__r**, and the **ambassad__r** congratulated the **swimm__r** on being the **winn__r** of the annual **riv__r** marathon swim.

8. Do I have your **permis__ion** to watch **televi__ion** during the **discus__ion** in your **man__ion**?

9. The **superstit__ous**, **invis__ble profess__r** was **miser__ble** during the **discus__ion** of the **aviat__r's glor__ous**, but **incred__ble** flight.

10. Was it an **illu__ion** or only a **rum__r** that the sounds of the **abomin__ble** snowman were **aud__ble** on the **expedi__ion** into the woods?

The Ultimate Homework Book © 2008 by Marvin Terban, Scholastic Teaching Resources

FIND THE HIDING ANTONYM!

Synonyms are words that have the same or almost the same meaning. **Bad, evil, villainous, nefarious,** and **dishonorable** are all synonyms.

Antonyms are words with opposite meanings. **Tall** and **short** are antonyms.

DIRECTIONS
In the list of 24 words below, 23 are synonyms. They all mean more or less the same thing as **good**. Hiding in the list is one word that doesn't belong because it means the opposite of the other words. It's an antonym! Find it and draw a line through it.

TiP
Keep a good dictionary, thesaurus, or dictionary of synonyms and antonyms nearby, or use one online to help you find the hiding word.

Synonyms for GOOD

admirable	fabulous	outstanding
awesome	fantastic	praiseworthy
commendable	fine	sterling
deplorable	first-rate	superb
estimable	laudable	superior
excellent	magnificent	terrific
exceptional	marvelous	wonderful
exemplary	meritorious	worthy

★ ★ ★ ★ ★ ★ ★ ★ ★ ★ ★

Find another synonym for **good**.

_____

The Ultimate Homework Book © 2008 by Marvin Terban, Scholastic Teaching Resources

ANTONYM, WHERE ARE YOU?

Synonyms are words that have the same or almost the same meaning. **Funny**, **humorous**, **hilarious**, **amusing**, and **comical** are all synonyms.

Antonyms are words with opposite meanings. **Silly** and **serious** are antonyms.

DIRECTIONS

In the list of 24 words below, 23 are synonyms. They all mean more or less same thing as **big**. Hiding in the list is one word that doesn't belong because it means the opposite of the other words. It's an antonym! Find it and draw a line through it.

TiP

Keep a good dictionary, thesaurus, or dictionary of synonyms and antonyms nearby, or use one online to help you find the hiding word.

Synonyms for BIG

astronomical	jumbo	sizable
colossal	mammoth	stupendous
elephantine	massive	substantial
enormous	minuscule	titanic
gargantuan	monstrous	towering
gigantic	monumental	tremendous
humongous	mountainous	vast
immense	prodigious	voluminous

Find another synonym for **big**.

_____

The Ultimate Homework Book © 2008 by Marvin Terban, Scholastic Teaching Resources

BE AN ANTONYM FINDER!

Synonyms are words that have the same or almost the same meaning. **Small, little, minute, tiny,** and **diminutive** are all synonyms.

Antonyms are words with opposite meanings. **Right** and **wrong** are antonyms.

DIRECTIONS

In the list of 24 words below, 23 are synonyms. They all mean more or less the same thing as **happy**. Hiding in the list is one word that doesn't belong because it means the opposite of the other words. It's an antonym! Find it and draw a line through it.

TiP
Keep a good dictionary, thesaurus, or dictionary of synonyms and antonyms nearby, or use one online to help you find the hiding word.

Synonyms for HAPPY

beaming	ecstatic	jovial
beatific	elated	joyous
blissful	euphoric	jubilant
blithe	exhilarated	lighthearted
buoyant	exultant	melancholy
carefree	gleeful	merry
cheerful	gratified	overjoyed
delighted	jolly	pleased

★ ★ ★ ★ ★ ★ ★ ★ ★ ★ ★

Find another synonym for **happy**.

_____

The Ultimate Homework Book © 2008 by Marvin Terban, Scholastic Teaching Resources

COME OUT, ANTONYM, WHEREVER YOU ARE!

Synonyms are words that have the same or almost the same meaning. **Silly**, **ridiculous**, **inane**, **foolish**, and **juvenile** are all synonyms.

Antonyms are words with opposite meanings. **Fast** and **slow** are antonyms.

DIRECTIONS

In the list of 24 words below, 23 are synonyms. They all mean more or less the same thing as **beautiful**. Hiding in the list is one word that doesn't belong because it means the opposite of the other words. It's an antonym! Find it and draw a line through it.

TiP
Keep a good dictionary, thesaurus, or dictionary of synonyms and antonyms nearby, or use one online to help you find the hiding word.

Synonyms for BEAUTIFUL

alluring	decorative	gorgeous
appealing	delightful	grotesque
attractive	elegant	handsome
beauteous	engaging	lovely
beguiling	exquisite	pretty
bewitching	fair	ravishing
charming	glamorous	stunning
comely	good-looking	winsome

★ ★ ★ ★ ★ ★ ★ ★ ★ ★ ★

Find another synonym for **beautiful**.

_____

The Ultimate Homework Book © 2008 by Marvin Terban, Scholastic Teaching Resources

YOU CAN'T HIDE FROM ME, ANTONYM!

Synonyms are words that have the same or almost the same meaning. **Clever**, **imaginative**, **inventive**, **ingenious**, and **resourceful** are all synonyms.

Antonyms are words with opposite meanings. **Hot** and **cold** are antonyms.

DIRECTIONS

In the list of 24 words below, 23 are synonyms. They all mean more or less the same thing as **intelligent**. Hiding in the list is one word that doesn't belong because it means the opposite of the other words. It's an antonym! Find it and draw a line through it.

TIP
Keep a good dictionary, thesaurus, or dictionary of synonyms and antonyms nearby, or use one online to help you find the hiding word.

Synonyms for INTELLIGENT

able	discerning	quick
astute	insightful	quick-witted
aware	intellectual	sagacious
brainy	intuitive	sharp
bright	knowledgeable	shrewd
brilliant	obtuse	smart
canny	perceptive	talented
clever	perspicacious	wise

★ ★ ★ ★ ★ ★ ★ ★ ★ ★ ★

Challenge

Find another synonym for **intelligent**.

_____

The Ultimate Homework Book © 2008 by Marvin Terban, Scholastic Teaching Resources

THERE'S THE ANTONYM!

Synonyms are words that have the same or almost the same meaning. **Smelly**, **stinking**, **reeking**, **putrid**, and **malodorous** are all synonyms.

Antonyms are words with opposite meanings. **Weak** and **strong** are antonyms.

DIRECTIONS
In the list of 24 words below, 23 are synonyms. They all mean more or less the same thing as **dirty**. Hiding in the list is one word that doesn't belong because it means the opposite of the other words. It's an antonym! Find it and draw a line through it.

> **TiP**
> Keep a good dictionary, thesaurus, or dictionary of synonyms and antonyms nearby, or use one online to help you find the hiding word.

Synonyms for DIRTY

befouled	grubby	smudged
begrimed	grungy	soiled
besmirched	hygienic	sooty
contaminated	impure	stained
defiled	mucky	sullied
filthy	muddy	tarnished
foul	polluted	unclean
grimy	smeared	unwashed

★ ★ ★ ★ ★ ★ ★ ★ ★ ★ ★

Find another synonym for **dirty**.

_____

The Ultimate Homework Book © 2008 by Marvin Terban, Scholastic Teaching Resources

GOTCHA, ANTONYM!

Synonyms are words that have the same or almost the same meaning. **Weird, strange, bizarre, odd,** and **peculiar** are all synonyms.

Antonyms are words with opposite meanings. **Open** and **closed** are antonyms.

DIRECTIONS

In the list of 24 words below, 23 are synonyms. They all mean more or less the same thing as **brave**. Hiding in the list is one word that doesn't belong because it means the opposite of the other words. It's an antonym! Find it and draw a line through it.

TiP

Keep a good dictionary, thesaurus, or dictionary of synonyms and antonyms nearby, or use one online to help you find the hiding word.

Synonyms for BRAVE

audacious	gutsy	spirited
courageous	heroic	spunky
daring	indomitable	stouthearted
dauntless	intrepid	unafraid
doughty	lionhearted	unflinching
fearless	mettlesome	unshrinking
gallant	plucky	valiant
game	pusillanimous	valorous

Challenge

Find another synonym for **brave**.

_____

The Ultimate Homework Book © 2008 by Marvin Terban, Scholastic Teaching Resources

THE OPPOSITES MACHINE

Synonyms are words that have the same or almost the same meaning. **Affluent**, **rich**, **prosperous**, and **well-to-do** are all synonyms.

Antonyms are words with opposite meanings. **Full** and **empty** are antonyms.

DIRECTIONS
Imagine you invented an "Opposites Machine."
If you put something in, it comes out its opposite. Put in something big, it comes out small. Choose carefully from the word list. Find antonyms of the words in the WHAT GOES IN column and write them in the appropriate spaces in the WHAT COMES OUT column.

TiP
Keep your favorite dictionary, thesaurus, or dictionary of synonyms and antonyms nearby. You'll probably need one of them.

WHAT GOES IN   WHAT COMES OUT

1. alarming ➔ _____
2. amiable ➔ _____
3. appalling ➔ _____
4. bogus ➔ _____
5. clumsy ➔ _____
6. complex ➔ _____
7. devious ➔ _____
8. fragrant ➔ _____
9. important ➔ _____
10. mammoth ➔ _____
11. monotonous ➔ _____
12. obscure ➔ _____
13. pernicious ➔ _____
14. real ➔ _____
15. reckless ➔ _____
16. traitorous ➔ _____
17. transparent ➔ _____
18. turbulent ➔ _____
19. uninterested ➔ _____
20. unsavory ➔ _____

WORD LIST

artificial
cautious
celebrated
cleansed
delectable
dexterous
disagreeable
fascinating
genuine
inquisitive
lovely
malodorous
meritorious
opaque
petite
simple
soothing
tranquil
trivial
trustworthy
truthful

The Ultimate Homework Book © 2008 by Marvin Terban, Scholastic Teaching Resources

CHANGE MY PET, DOC

Synonyms are words that have the same or almost the same meaning. **Greedy**, **gluttonous**, **voracious**, and **ravenous** are all synonyms.

Antonyms are words with opposite meanings. **Big** and **small** are antonyms.

DIRECTIONS
Imagine that you are a famous veterinarian who can work miracles with pets. People bring you animals they want to have transformed, and you can do it! From the group of words below, complete each sentence with an antonym of the word in boldface.

compassionate   genteel   industrious

svelte   virtuous   docile   handsome

ordinary   tame   youthful

> **TiP**
> Keep your favorite dictionary, thesaurus, or dictionary of synonyms and antonyms nearby. You'll probably need one of them.

1. My pet tortoise is so **antiquated** he can hardly move. Do you have anything that can make him more _____ ?

2. My cat's been acting **wicked** lately. I'd like a more _____ one.

3. My **wild** gerbil has been wrecking his new cage. Please do something to make him _____ .

4. My monkey is very **disobedient**. Change him into a _____ pet, please.

5. Isn't this animal **strange**? Do you have a more _____ one?

6. My pet canary is too **stout** for his cage. If he were _____ , he would fit in better.

7. My cat is very **lazy**. What can I do to make her more _____

8. Sometimes my pet tarantula can be **cruel**. Can you change him into a more _____ pet?

9. Everyone thinks my dog is **uncomely**. Do you have something that will make him more _____ ?

10. This boa constrictor is acting in a very **rude** manner. Can you train her to be more _____ ?

The Ultimate Homework Book © 2008 by Marvin Terban, Scholastic Teaching Resources

DEAR, YOU. PLEASE HELP!

Synonyms are words that have the same or almost the same meaning. **Timid**, **spineless**, **gutless**, and **cowardly** are all synonyms.

Antonyms are words with opposite meanings. **New** and **old** are antonyms.

DIRECTIONS

Imagine that you write a column for your school paper. People write you because they need advice about their relatives, friends, or even themselves! From the group of words below, complete each sentence with an antonym of the word in boldface.

> **TiP**
> Keep your favorite dictionary, thesaurus, or dictionary of synonyms and antonyms nearby. You'll probably need one of them.

affable   cautious   generous   modest   robust

affluent   frugal   humble   peaceable   sagacious

1. My brother is very **supercilious**. What can I do to make him more _____ ?

2. My grandpa sometimes feels **weak**. He wants to be more _____ . Can you help him?

3. My uncle is extremely **stingy** with his money. I need a more _____ uncle. Any suggestions?

4. My sister can be rather **foolish**. Could I trade her in for one who's really _____ ?

5. I don't get enough allowance, so I feel kind of **poor**. What can I do to become _____ ?

6. Sometimes my brother is **headstrong** and gets himself into trouble. How can I help him be _____ ?

7. My cousin is very **quarrelsome** sometimes. Is there a magic pill to make him _____ ?

8. My sister's new boyfriend is **arrogant** as can be. How can I convince her to find a more _____ guy?

9. My older sister needs to change her **lavish** lifestyle into something more _____ . What do you suggest?

10. Sometimes my friend acts like a **pompous** brat. Where can I find a pal who's more _____ ?

The Ultimate Homework Book © 2008 by Marvin Terban, Scholastic Teaching Resources

WELCOME TO THE FIX ANYTHING STORE

Synonyms are words that have the same or almost the same meaning. **Grand**, **majestic**, **splendid**, and **striking** are all synonyms.

Antonyms are words with opposite meanings. **High** and **low** are antonyms.

DIRECTIONS

Imagine that you own a store that can fix anything. People bring you all their stuff and you fix it in the way requested. From the group of words below, complete each sentence with an antonym of the word in boldface.

> **TiP**
> Keep your favorite dictionary, thesaurus, or dictionary of synonyms and antonyms nearby. You'll probably need one of them.

attractive   fascinating   melodious

buoyant   solid   faultless

fragrant   newfangled   sharp   valuable

1. Can you turn this **worthless** thingamajig into something _____ ?

2. This bouquet of flowers is **malodorous**. Can you spray something on it that will make it _____ ?

3. My bunk bed is so **flimsy** it keeps falling down. Fix it, please, so that it's _____ .

4. I can't hang this painting up because it's **unsightly**. Can you paint me an _____ one?

5. This book is **tedious**, and I fell asleep reading it. Can you please find me one that's _____ ?

6. This piano is too **heavy** to carry around. Do you have one that's _____ ?

7. My flute plays **discordant** music. I'd like it to be more _____ .

8. This camera is **defective**. I need one that's _____ to take pictures of my beautiful self.

9. This computer is **primitive**. Do you have something more _____ ?

10. My pencil point is too **blunt**. What can I do to make it very _____ ?

The Ultimate Homework Book © 2008 by Marvin Terban, Scholastic Teaching Resources

SAY ANYTHING BUT "SAY"!

A verb is a word that shows action or being. The verb **to say** is a very handy verb, especially when you're quoting people in a story. For example:

"I really love purple boots with pink polka dots," she **said**.

"Today is my pet elephant's birthday," he **said**.

But it can get boring saying "he said"/"she said" all the time. Luckily there are plenty of synonyms (words with the same meanings) for the verb **to say**.

For example, if someone speaks very softly, she could be **murmuring** or **purring**. If someone speaks loudly and angrily, you could use **to rant** or **to rage**.

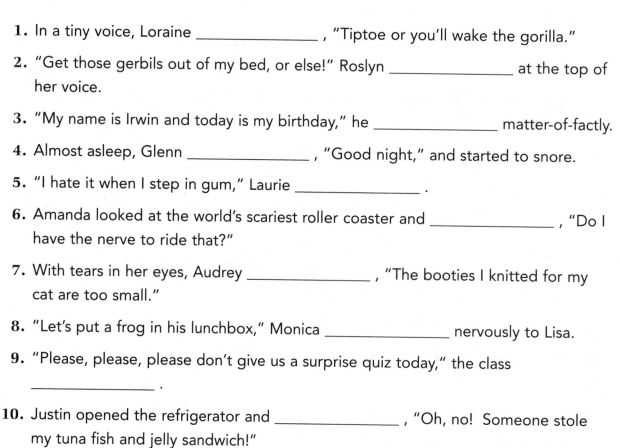

TIP
There are clues in the sentences that will help you choose the right verbs. If you're not certain about the exact meaning of a verb, check your dictionary.

DIRECTIONS
From the group of verbs below, choose a word to complete each sentence.

announced   giggled   mumbled   shouted   whispered

gasped   growled   pleaded   sobbed   wondered

1. In a tiny voice, Loraine _____ , "Tiptoe or you'll wake the gorilla."

2. "Get those gerbils out of my bed, or else!" Roslyn _____ at the top of her voice.

3. "My name is Irwin and today is my birthday," he _____ matter-of-factly.

4. Almost asleep, Glenn _____ , "Good night," and started to snore.

5. "I hate it when I step in gum," Laurie _____ .

6. Amanda looked at the world's scariest roller coaster and _____ , "Do I have the nerve to ride that?"

7. With tears in her eyes, Audrey _____ , "The booties I knitted for my cat are too small."

8. "Let's put a frog in his lunchbox," Monica _____ nervously to Lisa.

9. "Please, please, please don't give us a surprise quiz today," the class _____ .

10. Justin opened the refrigerator and _____ , "Oh, no! Someone stole my tuna fish and jelly sandwich!"

The Ultimate Homework Book © 2008 by Marvin Terban, Scholastic Teaching Resources

WHAT DO YOU ~~SAY~~ MUTTER ABOUT THAT?

A verb is a word that shows action or being. The verb **to say** is a very handy verb, especially when you're quoting people in a story. For example:

"I hid the jelly beans in the pencil sharpener," she **said**.

"Snow never fell in July before," he **said**.

But it can get boring saying "he said"/"she said" all the time. Luckily there are plenty of synonyms (words with the same meanings) for the verb **to say**.

For example, if someone speaks very softly, she could be **murmuring** or **purring**. If someone speaks loudly and angrily, you could use **to rant** or **to rage**.

> **TIP**
> There are clues in the sentences that will help you choose the right verbs. If you're not certain about the exact meaning of a verb, check your dictionary.

DIRECTIONS
From the group of verbs below, choose a word to complete each sentence.

barked   blubbered   declared   inquired   sighed
begged   chuckled   hissed   protested   threatened

1. "Dance with the chicken now, or you're fired!" the angry boss _____ .

2. Jade looked sadly at his picture and softly _____ , "If I had married him, my life would be different today."

3. "This is my land, and you're trespassing, " George _____ forcefully.

4. Noisily, and like a little child, she _____ , "I don't like that candy."

5. "Get off the stage! You can't sing," the rude audience _____ .

6. With a questioning look in her blue eyes, Bonnie _____ , "Is this where they sell the orange cactuses?"

7. "Don't punish him, Dad," the princess _____ earnestly. "He didn't know I was your daughter."

8. With a small grin on his face, Aaron _____ to himself, "That will teach him not to borrow my asparagus."

9. "It isn't true that I drank all the milkshakes!" Jessica _____ loudly.

10. Kurt raised his fist and _____ , "Talk that way again to my parakeet, and you'll have to deal with me!"

The Ultimate Homework Book © 2008 by Marvin Terban, Scholastic Teaching Resources

PLAY WITH "SAY"

A verb is a word that shows action or being. The verb **to say** is a very handy verb, especially when you're quoting people in a story. For example:

"This elevator goes up, not down," she **said**.

"Her shoes were made of coconuts," he **said**.

But it can get boring saying "he said"/"she said" all the time. Luckily there are plenty of synonyms (words with the same meanings) for the verb **to say**.

For example, if someone speaks very softly, she could be **murmuring** or **purring**. If someone speaks loudly and angrily, you could use **to rant** or **to rage**.

> **TiP**
> There are clues in the sentences that will help you choose the right verbs. If you're not certain about the exact meaning of a verb, check your dictionary.

DIRECTIONS

From the group of verbs below, choose a word to complete each sentence.

argued   beseeched   asked   reported   urged
demanded   cheered   fumed   teased   whined

1. "Oh, I'll bet you're too scared to shake hands with this nice gorilla," Jennifer _____ playfully.

2. "We won the championship!" _____ the girls.

3. "Give that back to me right now!" David _____ .

4. The messenger approached the king and _____ , "The enemy has retreated, your majesty."

5. "This is the most outrageous thing I have ever heard in my life!" the principal angrily _____ .

6. Karen went up to the man with the beard and _____ , "Is there an ATM machine around here somewhere?"

7. "Queen, queen, don't cut off my golden locks," Cindy _____ .

8. "Everything's going wrong. Today is a terrible day for me," he _____ .

9. "The Atlantic is a much nicer ocean than the Pacific," John _____ .

10. "Wear a helmet when you ride your bike," his grandma _____ .

The Ultimate Homework Book © 2008 by Marvin Terban, Scholastic Teaching Resources

ARE THEY SYNONYM OR ANTONYM VERBS?

Synonyms are words that have the same meaning.

Antonyms are words that have opposite meanings.

A verb is a word that shows action.

TiP
Keep a dictionary or thesaurus nearby. You might need it.

DIRECTIONS
In the space in front of each pair of verbs below, print **S** if the words are synonyms, **A** if they're antonyms.

1. ____ **cease** and **stop**

2. ____ **create** and **obliterate**

3. ____ **mistreat** and **abuse**

4. ____ **accomplish** and **achieve**

5. ____ **captivate** and **repel**

6. ____ **deceive** and **mislead**

7. ____ **pursue** and **avoid**

8. ____ **insist** and **concede**

9. ____ **protect** and **shield**

10. ____ **unite** and **sever**

The Ultimate Homework Book © 2008 by Marvin Terban, Scholastic Teaching Resources

ARE THEY SYNONYM OR ANTONYMS ADVERBS?

Synonyms are words that have the same meaning.

Antonyms are words that have opposite meanings.

An adverb is a word that usually answers the question "how?" about a verb. It often ends with the letters -ly.

TiP
Keep a dictionary or thesaurus nearby. You might need it.

DIRECTIONS

In the space in front of each pair of adverbs below, print **S** if the words are synonyms, **A** if they're antonyms.

1. ___ **energetically** and **lethargically**

2. ___ **hideously** and **disgustingly**

3. ___ **cheerfully** and **miserably**

4. ___ **thunderously** and **faintly**

5. ___ **brilliantly** and **unwisely**

6. ___ **comically** and **humorously**

7. ___ **opulently** and **affluently**

8. ___ **rapidly** and **sluggishly**

9. ___ **garrulously** and **verbosely**

10. ___ **tranquilly** and **serenely**

The Ultimate Homework Book © 2008 by Marvin Terban, Scholastic Teaching Resources

ARE THEY SYNONYM OR ANTONYM NOUNS?

Synonyms are words that have the same meaning.

Antonyms are words that have opposite meanings.

A noun is a word that names a person, place, thing, or idea.

TiP
Keep a dictionary or thesaurus nearby. You might need it.

DIRECTIONS
In the space in front of each pair of nouns below, print **S** if the words are synonyms, **A** if they're antonyms.

1. ____ **pupil** and **student**

2. ____ **veracity** and **dishonesty**

3. ____ **wages** and **remuneration**

4. ____ **calamity** and **disaster**

5. ____ **frailty** and **weakness**

6. ____ **agreement** and **discord**

7. ____ **competition** and **rivalry**

8. ____ **folly** and **imprudence**

9. ____ **courage** and **cowardice**

10. ____ **elation** and **dejection**

The Ultimate Homework Book © 2008 by Marvin Terban, Scholastic Teaching Resources

ARE THEY SYNONYM OR ANTONYMS ADJECTIVES?

Synonyms are words that have the same meaning.

Antonyms are words that have opposite meanings.

An adjective is a word that describes a noun.

TiP
Keep a dictionary or thesaurus nearby. You might need it.

DIRECTIONS
In the space in front of each pair of adjectives below, print **S** if the words are synonyms, **A** if they're antonyms.

1. ____ **normal** and **exceptional**

2. ____ **corpulent** and **skinny**

3. ____ **flexible** and **lithe**

4. ____ **insufferable** and **tolerable**

5. ____ **deleterious** and **harmful**

6. ____ **arrogant** and **haughty**

7. ____ **recalcitrant** and **obedient**

8. ____ **frail** and **feeble**

9. ____ **hot** and **frigid**

10. ____ **pacific** and **calm**

The Ultimate Homework Book © 2008 by Marvin Terban, Scholastic Teaching Resources

FILL IN THE MISSING SYNONYMS

Synonyms are words that have the same meaning.

Antonyms are words that have opposite meanings.

DIRECTIONS

In each block of four boxes below there are three synonyms. From the group of words below, find another synonym and finish the block by writing that word in the last box.

TiP
Keep a dictionary or thesaurus nearby. You might need it.

| assiduous | constantly | maladroit | rash | thwart |
| confuse | diffident | radiant | rational | vile |

1.	reckless	foolhardy	hasty	
2.	sensible	reasonable	judicious	
3.	prevent	obstruct	hinder	
4.	diligent	industrious	sedulous	
5.	contemptible	despicable	disreputable	
6.	continually	persistently	repeatedly	
7.	awkward	clumsy	ungainly	
8.	confound	babble	perplex	
9.	bashful	modest	shy	
10.	shining	beaming	gleaming	

The Ultimate Homework Book © 2008 by Marvin Terban, Scholastic Teaching Resources

FILL IN THE MISSING ANTONYMS

Synonyms are words that have the same meaning.

Antonyms are words that have opposite meanings.

DIRECTIONS
In each block of four boxes below there are three synonyms. From the group of words below, find an antonym and finish the block by writing that word in the last box.

TiP
Keep a dictionary or thesaurus nearby. You might need it.

awake   expand   heal   ineffective   prolixity
exonerate   fondness   indifferent   misery   timid

1.	blame	censure	rebuke	
2.	fracture	break	rend	
3.	conciseness	succinctness	brevity	
4.	bliss	joy	rapture	
5.	fearless	bold	dauntless	
6.	loathing	aversion	dislike	
7.	dormant	slumbering	quiescent	
8.	dwindle	diminish	decrease	
9.	eager	ardent	determined	
10.	influential	powerful	controlling	

The Ultimate Homework Book © 2008 by Marvin Terban, Scholastic Teaching Resources

THE SYNONYM ADVERTISING AGENCY

Synonyms are words that have the same meaning.

Antonyms are words that have opposite meanings.

DIRECTIONS
Imagine you work for a big advertising agency. Somebody has already started to write the ads but your job is to write one more synonym to complete them. Choose from the group of words below.

benevolent	clamorous	gripping	luscious	salubrious
bucolic	comfortable	insolent	sagacious	unruly

1. This new action-adventure book from **Riveting** Books, Inc., is **fascinating, engrossing**, and _____ .

2. Eating fruits and vegetables from **Healthy** Farms is **wholesome, nourishing**, and _____ .

3. The Feline Obedience School will turn your **rude, impertinent**, and _____ kitty into a sweetie cat.

4. Furniture from the **Restful** Furniture Company will make your living room feel **cozy, snug**, and _____ .

5. The **Scrumptious** Diner offers **delicious, flavorful**, and _____ meals.

6. Let the **compassionate, kindhearted**, and _____ people at the **Humane** Helpers Society solve your problems.

7. Trust your money to **Intelligent** Investors Corporation because we're **shrewd, sharp**, and _____ .

8. Tough Tiger Babysitting Service handles all kinds of **obstreperous, rowdy**, and _____ children.

9. Anti-**Sonorous** Systems will quiet your **noisy, loud**, and _____ office or home.

10. Tired of city living? Let **Countryside** Real Estate introduce you to a **rural, pastoral**, and _____ lifestyle.

The Ultimate Homework Book © 2008 by Marvin Terban, Scholastic Teaching Resources

LITTLE INTO BIG

Synonyms are words that have the same meaning.

Antonyms are words that have opposite meanings.

DIRECTIONS

Imagine you invented a machine that turns little words (5 letters or less) into big words with exactly the same meanings. From the group of words below, choose words that will change the little words into big words. Got your dictionary or thesaurus nearby?

| accelerated | euphoric | iniquitous | outstanding | scorching |
| disconsolate | gargantuan | minuscule | percipient | sluggardly |

LITTLE WORDS	CHANGED INTO	BIG WORDS
1. good	→ → → → → → → → →	_____
2. bad	→ → → → → → → → →	_____
3. small	→ → → → → → → → →	_____
4. big	→ → → → → → → → →	_____
5. happy	→ → → → → → → → →	_____
6. sad	→ → → → → → → → →	_____
7. fast	→ → → → → → → → →	_____
8. slow	→ → → → → → → → →	_____
9. smart	→ → → → → → → → →	_____
10. hot	→ → → → → → → → →	_____

The Ultimate Homework Book © 2008 by Marvin Terban, Scholastic Teaching Resources

BUTTERFLY FLUTTERS BY

Some animals move on four legs, some on two. Some animals have no legs at all. Some have wings to fly through the sky. Some have fins to swim through the water. There are many good verbs that tell how animals move.

DIRECTIONS

From the list of words below, select the best verbs to complete the sentences.

burrow	dive	jump	soar	swing	climb	gallop
run	squirm	swoop	crawl	hop	slither	swim	waddle

1. Every Saturday in the park we watch horses _____ around the track.

2. On our trip to Australia we loved to observe the kangaroos _____ .

3. The penguins at the zoo _____ along and make every smile.

4. We went out into the yard and saw worms _____ along the ground.

5. In the jungle I watched snakes _____ silently across the jungle floor.

6. Majestically the eagles _____ high up into the sky.

7. Moles can _____ as much as a foot per minute into the ground.

8. Hundreds of fish _____ past you in this river every minute.

9. We laughed seeing the monkeys _____ from branch to branch.

10. How awesome whales are when they _____ deep into the ocean.

11. Spiders love to _____ all around their sticky webs.

12. In the park we saw squirrels _____ rapidly up the sides of trees.

13. Falcons _____ from great heights and catch pray with their talons.

14. A tiny flea can _____ 100 times its height.

15. Cheetahs, the fastest creatures on land, _____ at lightning speeds.

The Ultimate Homework Book © 2008 by Marvin Terban, Scholastic Teaching Resources

YOU'RE WEIRD, VERBS!

A verb is a word that shows action or being.

Usually you just add **-ed** or **-d** to change a verb from the present to the past tense. All regular verbs do that. For example:

Present tense	Now I **walk**.
Past tense	Yesterday I **walked**.

Some verbs are irregular. They form their past tenses in ways that you might not expect. For example:

Present tense	Today I **get** on the bus.
Past tense	Yesterday I **got** off the bus.

DIRECTIONS

Fill in the empty boxes below with the correct past tenses of some common irregular verbs. Remember, they won't end with the letters **-ed**.

NOW I . . .
(present tense)

YESTERDAY I . . .
(past tense)

1. choose a friend _____
2. do my homework _____
3. eat my snack _____
4. get the message _____
5. know the answer _____
6. leave my house _____
7. lose the keys _____
8. meet my sister _____
9. pay the money _____
10. rise from my chair _____
11. run a race _____
12. see the movie _____
13. sit on the bench _____
14. slide on the ice _____
15. take the advice _____

The Ultimate Homework Book © 2008 by Marvin Terban, Scholastic Teaching Resources

STRANGE VERBS

A verb is a word that shows action or being.

Usually you just add **-ed** or **-d** to change a verb from the present to the past tense. All regular verbs do that. For example:

Present tense	Now I **walk**.
Past tense	Yesterday I **walked**.

Some verbs are irregular. They form their past tenses in ways that you might not expect. For example:

Present tense	Today I **get** on the bus.
Past tense	Yesterday I **got** off the bus.

DIRECTIONS

In each sentence below, three verbs are in boldface, but only one is the correct past tense. Circle the correct word. Be careful. Some are very tricky.

1. My brother (**taked took tooked**) all the cherries from the top of the sundae and gave me the rest of the dessert.

2. I (**bited bat bit**) into the hard bagel and almost cracked my new tooth.

3. When he (**broke breaked bruke**) my favorite statue of the hippo ballerina, I thought I would faint.

4. As soon as he (**camed commed came**) out of his cage, I knew he was the tarantula for me.

5. First I (**writ wrote writed**) him a goodbye e-mail; then I called him to say "hello."

6. The illustrator who visited our school (**drew drawed drewed**) a picture.

7. Last week I (**shaked shook shuk**) the hand of my favorite TV star.

8. I almost (**freezed friz froze**) my nose off last night waiting for you outside.

9. My sister (**swimmed swam swum**) the lake in one minute when she thought a shark was following her.

10. The floor was so slippery that he (**slid slided sled**) all the way across the room.

The Ultimate Homework Book © 2008 by Marvin Terban, Scholastic Teaching Resources

WHAT'S THE PAST?

A verb is a word that shows action or being.

Usually you just add **-ed** or **-d** to change a verb from the present to the past tense. All regular verbs do that. For example:

Present tense	Now I **walk**.
Past tense	Yesterday I **walked**.

Some verbs are irregular. They form their past tenses in ways that you might not expect. For example:

Present tense	Today I **get** on the bus.
Past tense	Yesterday I **got** off the bus.

DIRECTIONS

In front of each sentence below there is an irregular verb in boldface. Complete the sentence with the past tense of that verb. Remember, the past tenses of irregular verbs are very tricky.

1. (**wear**) Karen _____ the monkey costume in the play and looked great in it!

2. (**tell**) I _____ you not to play with my pet boa constrictor because it hugs too hard.

3. (**strive**) My uncle always _____ to be the best, and he became the world's loudest yodeler.

4. (**speak**) When he softly _____ the words "Ish ka bibble," she started to dance the Funky Chicken.

5. (**shoot**) William Tell _____ an arrow into an apple on top of his son's head.

6. (**rise**) The sea serpent _____ unexpectedly from the little pond and asked where Buffalo was.

7. (**lose**) If you _____ your lunchbox, I'll gladly share my lunch with you.

8. (**grow**) Jack planted the magic seeds and they _____ into a giant beanstalk.

9. (**drive**) The farmer _____ his horse and wagon to the market to buy some jelly beans for his pig.

10. (**bind**) The nurse didn't have any bandages left, so she _____ the wound with ribbons.

The Ultimate Homework Book © 2008 by Marvin Terban, Scholastic Teaching Resources

OUGHT IT BE AUGHT?

The past tense of some irregular verbs ends with -**aught** and others with -**ought**. There's no really good reason for this. They just do.

DIRECTIONS

What are the past tenses of the irregular verbs below? Do they end with -**aught** or -**ought**? Put **a** or **o** on the blank lines in the words below.

1. Now I **buy** a berserk baboon.

   Yesterday I **b___ught** one.

2. Now I **fight** a ferocious frog.

   Last week I **f___ught** one.

3. Now I **catch** a cuddly crocodile.

   A week ago I **c___ught** one.

4. Now I **bring** a bragging brontosaurus.

   Last Monday I **br___ught** one.

5. Now I **teach** tumbling turtles.

   In 1897 I **t___ught** them.

6. Now I **seek** singing seals.

   The day before Thursday I **s___ught** them.

7. Now I **think** about things.

   Once upon a time, I **th___ught** about them.

8. Now I **buy** a pie for the guy.

   For his last birthday, I **b___ught** one.

9. Now I **bring** a ring to the king.

   Last week I **br___ught** him one.

10. Now I **think** about the pink sink.

    Last year I **th___ught** it was a good idea to buy one.

The Ultimate Homework Book © 2008 by Marvin Terban, Scholastic Teaching Resources

-ANG OR -UNG?

If an irregular verb ends with **-ing** in the present tense, the letter **i** sometimes changes to **a** and sometimes to **u** in the past tense. That can be tricky.

DIRECTIONS
Put **ang** or **ung** on the blank lines to complete the past-tense verbs below.

TIP
There's a trick on this page. One of the verbs is not **-ang** or **-ung** in its past tense. Which one is it? Don't be fooled.

1. Now I **sting** like a bumblebee.

   Yesterday I **st**_____ like one.

2. Now I **spring** from my seat.

   Yesterday I **spr**_____ from it.

3. Now I **cling** to my teddy bear.

   Yesterday I **cl**_____ to it.

4. Now I **fling** the ball into the air.

   Yesterday I **fl**_____ it.

5. Now I **ring** the bell loudly.

   Yesterday I **r**_____ it.

6. Now I **wring** out my bathing suit.

   Yesterday I **wr**_____ it out.

7. Now I **bring** my bunny a bun.

   Yesterday I **br**_____ her one.

8. Now I **sing** a song of sixpence.

   Yesterday I **s**_____ it.

The Ultimate Homework Book © 2008 by Marvin Terban, Scholastic Teaching Resources

STAY-THE-SAME VERBS!

A few irregular verbs don't change their spellings or their pronunciations at all when they go from the present tense to the past tense.

DIRECTIONS

In the paragraph below there are 11 irregular verbs in the past tense. All of them are in boldface. Five of the verbs are the same in the present tense as they are in the past tense. (They're really irregular!) Circle those five verbs.

TiP

To figure out which verbs are the same in the present and past tenses, say "Now I" and the present tense of a verb, and then say "Yesterday I" and the past tense of the same verb. You'll discover which ones don't change. If not, grab a dictionary.

Last Tuesday, Cousin Bertha **burst** through the door and shouted, "I just **tore** my dress on a cactus needle!" There she **stood**, as the sun **shone** brightly on her ripped dress. She **dove** into her toy box, took out a tin drum, and **beat** it vigorously, all the while singing, "No more cactus needles!" Then she **cut** off the end of a carrot and **began** chewing it. Before the sun **set** that day, Cousin Bertha **rid** our yard of cactus needles. Then she **slept** for 12 hours.

The past tense of most irregular verbs have some of the same letters as the present tense. For example, **speak** (present tense) becomes **spoke** (past tense). But one irregular verb changes its spelling entirely in the past tense. There are no letters in the past tense that are in the present tense. Can you guess what it is? What are the present and past tenses of this verb?

Present tense: _____

Past tense: _____

HiNT
It means "to move from one place to another," and it rhymes with *glow*.

The Ultimate Homework Book © 2008 by Marvin Terban, Scholastic Teaching Resources

IRREGULAR VERB HOMONYMS

The past tenses of some irregular verbs sound like, or almost like, other words. They're spelled differently, though.

Sometimes words that look as if they should rhyme don't. It can be confusing. For example:

> The past tense of **say** is **said** and it rhymes with **red**.
>
> The past tense of **pay** is **paid** and it rhymes with **raid**.

TiP
Remember to read each clue.

DIRECTIONS

See if you can figure out what the verbs and their sound-alikes are. Write them in the empty boxes. The first one has been done for you.

	PAST TENSE	SOUND-ALIKES
1. The past tense of **eat** Sound-alike: The number after seven	ate	eight
2. The past tense of **blow** Sound-alike: The color of the sky		
3. The past tense of **fly** Sound-alikes: Short form of influenza, a duct to let out smoke		
4. The past tense of **know** Sound-alike: Large antelope (wildebeest)		
5. The past tense of **read** Sound-alike: The color of a strawberry		
6. The past tense of **ride** Sound-alikes: The past tense of row, a surfaced route for vehicles		
7. The past tense of **wring** Sound-alike: A step on a ladder		
8. The past tense of **tell** Sound-alike: The past tense of toll		
9. The past tense of **throw** Sound-alike: In one side and out the other		
10. The past tense of **write** Sound-alike: Repetition of a thing to learn it		

The Ultimate Homework Book © 2008 by Marvin Terban, Scholastic Teaching Resources

ANSWERS

Page 11:
1. Dr., Dr.
2. Jr.
3. qt.
4. Ph.D.
5. Inc.
6. vs.
7. cm.
8. Dept.
9. Mr., Mrs.
10. Prof.

Page 12:
1. ante meridiem
2. as soon as possible
3. American Society for the Prevention of Cruelty to Animals
4. Bachelor of Arts
5. Central Intelligence Agency
6. collect (or cash) on delivery
7. Federal Bureau of Investigation
8. miles per hour
9. National Basketball Association
10. personal computer
11. post meridiem
12. post office
13. registered nurse
14. Repondez s'il vous plait
15. recreational vehicle
16. tender loving care
17. very important person

Page 13:
1. Alabama; AL, AK
2. Arkansas; AR, AZ
3. Colorado; CO, CT
4. Massachusetts; ME, MD, MA
5. Michigan; MI, MN, MS, MO
6. Nebraska; NE, NV

Page 14:
1. AL, 2. AK, 3. CO, 4. FL, 5. GA, 6. HI, 7. ID, 8. IL, 9. IN, 10. IA, 11. KS, 12. KY, 13. LA, 14. ME, 15. MD, 16. MA, 17. MI,

18. NE, 19. OH, 20. OK, 21. OR, 22. PA, 23. UT, 24. VT, 25. VA, 26. WA, 27. WI, 28. WY
Challenge: California, CA; Colorado, CO; Delaware, DE

Page 15:
1. AK, 2. AZ, 3. MN, 4. MS, 5. MO, 6. MT, 7. NV, 8. NH, 9. NJ, 10. NM, 11. NY, 12. NC, 13. ND, 14. RI ,15. SC, 16. SD, 17. TN, 18. TX, 19. WV

Page 16:
1. HI, Hawaii
2. IN, Indiana
3. ME, Maine
4. MD, Maryland
5. MA, Massachusetts
6. PA, Pennsylvania
7. OR, Oregon
8. OK, Oklahoma
9. MI, Michigan
10. LA, Louisiana

Page 17:
1. HI, MA. HI, PA.
2. MA OR PA.
3. ME OK.
4. DR. MA.
5. IN PA.

Page 18:
1. COAL, Colorado, Alabama
2. HIDE, Hawaii, Delaware
3. MANE, Massachusetts, Nebraska
4. LANE, Louisiana, Nebraska
5. MEAL, Maine, Alabama
6. PAID, Pennsylvania, Idaho
7. HIND, Hawaii, North Dakota
8. MOOR, Missouri, Oregon
9. PAIN, Pennsylvania, Indiana

10. CANE, California, Nebraska
11. MEND, Maine, North Dakota
12. RIDE, Rhode Island, Delaware
13. CODE, Colorado, Delaware
14. LAND Louisiana, North Dakota
15. VANE Virginia, Nebraska
16. RIND Rhode Island, North Dakota

Page 19:
1. c, 2. e, 3. j, 4. s, 5. d, 6. g, 7. h, 8. k, 9. o, 10. b, 11. n, 12. m, 13. l, 14. r, 15. p, 16. a, 17. i, 18. q, 19. f

Page 20:
1. R, 2. F, 3. R, 4. F, 5. R, 6. R, 7. R, 8. R, 9. R, 10. F, 11. R, 12. R, 13. R, 14. F, 15. R, 16. R, 17. R, 18. R, 19. R, 20. F, 21. R, 22. R, 23. R, 24. R, 25. R, 26. R, 27. F, 28. R, 29. R, 30. F

Page 21:
1. smarter
2. more glamorous
3. heavier
4. more mouthwatering
5. messier
6. funnier
7. more frightening
8. more colossal

Page 22:
1. prettiest
2. longest
3. softest
4. most ferocious
5. happiest
6. most intelligent
7. sweetest
8. most amazing

Page 23:
1. better, best
2. worse, worst
3. more, most

4. less, least
5. more, most

Page 24:
1. ursine
2. bubaline
3. taurine
4. cameline
5. galline
6. bovine
7. crocodilian
8. canine
9. delphine
10. elephantine
11. piscine
12. vulpine
13. ranine
14. giraffine
15. equine
16. leonine
17. octopine
18. porcine
19. reptilian
20. serpentine
Challenge: human

Page 25:
1. French
2. Chinese
3. Australian
4. Swiss
5. Victorian
6. Mexican
7. Elizabethan
8. Martian
9. Peruvian
10. Irish

Page 26:
1. ADJ., CHILLY
2. ADV., HAPPILY
3. ADJ., SMELLY
4. ADV., LOUDLY
5. ADJ., ELDERLY
6. ADJ., UGLY
7. ADV., FOOLISHLY
8. ADJ., CURLY
9. ADV., BOLDLY
10. ADJ., CUDDLY

Page 27:
1. swift, swiftly
2. beautiful, beautifully
3. honestly, honest
4. quick, quickly
5. loud, loudly

6. shortly, short
7. softly, soft
8. sweet, sweetly
9. bad, badly
10. wisely, wise

Page 28:
1. noisily
2. hard
3. tidily
4. fast
5. hungrily
6. hastily
7. well
8. late
9. sensibly
10. angrily

Page 29:
The following words
should be circled:
busily, effortlessly,
wildly, easily,
enthusiastically, rapidly,
elegantly, loudly,
gracefully, quickly,
excitedly, hilariously,
triumphantly, beautifully,
happily

Page 30:
1. how
2. when
3. where
4. when
5. how
6. where
7. when
8. how
9. where
10. how

Page 31:
Answers may vary.
Sample answers:
1. quite
2. exceptionally
3. incredibly
4. truly
5. really
6. terribly
7. tremendously
8. enormously
9. extraordinarily
10. extremely

Page 32:
1. Roosevelt
2. Washington

3. Pierce
4. Madison
5. Monroe
6. Adams
7. Van Buren
8. Harrison
9. Hayes
10. Garfield
11. McKinley
12. Wilson
13. Truman
14. Reagan

Page 33:
1. girl's
2. dog's, goose's
3. Mr. Thomas's
4. ox's, cow's
5. baby's, people's
6. deer's
7. Dennis's, Mr.
Schwartz's
8. girl's, sister's
9. class's, school's
10. mouse's

Page 34:
1. birds, birds' feathers
2. moose, moose's hooves
3. artists, artists'
paintbrushes
4. foxes, foxes' tracks
5. brothers, brothers'
clothes
6. geese, geese's beaks
7. pilots, pilots' union
8. children, children's
toys
9. women, women's coats
10. sheep, sheep's food

Page 35:
1. dragon's, queen's
2. soldiers'
3. kids', mother's
4. president's, brother's
5. Liz's, Harris's
6. oxen's
7. ladies', men's
8. cousin's, children's
9. Suzy's, gerbil's
10. Mrs. Diaz's, boss's

Page 36:
1. I'm
2. we've
3. He's
4. she'll
5. we're

6. won't
7. That'll
8. couldn't
9. There's
10. mustn't

Page 37:
1. wasn't
2. you've
3. hasn't
4. didn't
5. shouldn't
6. You'd
7. wouldn't
8. it'll
9. aren't
10. I'd

Page 38:
1. it's, its
2. Your, you're
3. who's, whose
4. heel, he'll, heal
5. heed, he'd
6. we'd, weed
7. lets, let's
8. We'll, wheel
9. They're, there, their
10. I'll, aisle, isle

Page 39:
1. Idaho, Maine, Audrey
2. At, Museum,
European, Art, Dutch
3. Thomas, Edison
4. If, I, I, I,
5. Do, Chinese, Japanese,
Mexican
6. The, American,
Charlie, Chaplin, London
7. The, Spain, I, Spanish
8. Things, Thailand, Thai,
Switzerland, Swiss

Page 40:
1. Grandmother,
Freedman, Cousin,
Laurie
2. Tomorrow, Mother, I'll,
Richard, Farnsworth, Esq.
3. Is, Grandma, Shirley,
Uncle, Lewis's
4. Dad, Dr., Timothy,
James, Williams, Long,
Island
5. That's, Aunt, Bonnie,
Kurt, Westerman, Sr.,
Iceland
6. Please, Grandfather

7. Mom, Dad
8. Franklin, Roosevelt, Jr.

Page 41:
1. At, School, Brilliant,
Babies, I, Chinese
2. My, Northwest,
Southeast
3. My, Kilmer, College,
Laughable, Literature
4. People, Easter, Sunday
5. They, Arabic, Amharic,
African, Folk, Festival
6. You, Swedish, Sweden,
Swings
7. Yom, Kippur, Good,
Friday
8. Curiously, Winter,
Wonderland, Fair

Page 42:
1. The, Saturn
2. Franklin, Declaration,
Independence,
Constitution
3. Please, Cheerios,
Kleenex, Scotch Tape
4. My, Depression,
Korean, War
5. I, Goodyear, General,
Motors
6. Genesis, Ecclesiastes,
Exodus, Leviticus, Bible
7. We, Boston, Tea, Party,
Battle, Bunker, Hill
8. Venus, I'll, Earth

Page 43:
1. The, United, Nations,
Swahili, Tsonga, Zulu
2. They're, Starbucks,
Radio, Shack
3. Did, Peanut
4. Which, Japanese,
Chinese, Vietnamese
5. Are, Gap, Macy's
6. Do, McDonald's,
Wendy's, Burger, King
7. Some, Italian
Americans, Italian,
English
8. My, You're
9. Christians, Muslims,
Hindus, Buddhists, Jews
10. Lincoln, Fourscore

Page 44:
1. Mrs., Consuela,
Schlepkis, Miss, Karen,
Youngman

Answers

2. In, Gone, With, Wind
3. I, Thursday, Sunday
4. My, The, History, World
5. Dr., Christiaan, Barnard
6. I, The, Sound, Music, The, Wizard, Oz
7. Capt., Edward, Heroic, Heroes
8. Prof., Piano, The, Star-Spangled, Banner, Monday
9. On, Saturdays, Mr., W., T., James, The, Daily, Bugle
10. I, A, Lovely, Life, Monday

Page 45:
The following words should be capitalized in the first exercise:
Dear, Party, Decoration, Committee, I, Halloween, October, Pumpkins, Thank, Yours, Henry, J., Artsy
The following words should be capitalized in the second exercise:
Dear, Customer, Service, Department, I, Zippy, August, I, September, How, I, Gratefully, Miss, Isla, Ubiles

Page 46:
1. haircut
2. grasshopper
3. flashlight
4. bloodhound
5. cowboy
6. goldfish
7. notebook
8. toothbrush
9. wristwatch
10. snowstorm

Page 47:
1. basketball
2. classmate
3. firehouse
4. rowboat
5. landlord
6. flowerpot
7. clipboard
8. motorcycle
9. gentleman
10. washcloth

Page 48:
1. blackboard
2. earthquake
3. sunbeam
4. drugstore
5. wastebasket
6. watchdog
7. campfire
8. sandpaper
9. rattlesnake
10. cupcake

Page 49:
1. dragonfly
2. highchair
3. jellybean
4. eyeball
5. lifeguard
6. outfield
7. pigtail
8. rainbow
9. popcorn
10. password

Page 50:
1. flagpole
2. overcoat
3. railroad
4. crosswalk
5. handlebar
6. waterfall
7. headache
8. shoelace
9. bathroom
10. shipwreck

Page 51:
1. but
2. and
3. or
4. and
5. or
6. but
7. and
8. or
9. but
10. or

Page 52:
1. Pantaloon (pants)
2. Jules Léotard (leotard)
3. Amelia J. Bloomer (bloomers)
4. Lord Cardigan (cardigan)
5. Levi Strauss, (Levi's®)
6. Bikini Atoll, (bikini)

Page 53:
1. Hamburg, Germany (hamburger)
2. Sylvester Graham (Graham cracker)
3. Cheddar, England (cheddar cheese)
4. Bologna, Italy (bologna/baloney)
5. Earl of Sandwich (sandwich)
6. Frankfurt, Germany (frankfurter)

Page 54:
1. Robert Bunsen (Bunsen burner)
2. Louis Braille (Braille)
3. Joseph Guillotin (guillotine)
4. Antoine J. Sax (saxophone)
5. George W. Ferris (Ferris wheel)
6. Theodore Roosevelt (teddy bear)

Page 55:
1. loafer
2. mobster
3. waiter
4. caramel
5. weaver
6. tycoon
7. scale
8. manager
9. monster
10. chickpea

Page 56:
1. muffin
2. mustard
3. battle
4. pants
5. toenail
6. balloon
7. musketeer
8. cantaloupe
9. truck
10. crayon

Page 57:
1. Polish: zzzzz
2. Thai: jip jip
3. Japanese: nyan nyan
4. Danish: klook klook
5. Korean: um-moo
6. Italian: cree cree
7. Greek: kra kra

8. French: wah wah
9. Farsi: eee haw
10. German: maaaaa maaaaa
11. Swedish: twee twee
12. Hebrew: cleek cleek
13. Russian: hru hru
14. Spanish: kee-kee-ree-kee
15. Chinese: goo goo

Page 58:
1. goody-goody
2. cha-cha
3. ha-ha
4. hush-hush
5. no-no
6. pom-pom
7. so-so
8. tutu
9. yo-yo
10. yum-yum
11. rah-rah
12. buddy-buddy

Page 59:
1. chitchat
2. clickety-clack
3. clippety-clop
4. dilly-dally
5. dingdong
6. doodad
7. hee-haw
8. hippety-hop
9. ho-hum
10. hunky-dory
11. jibber-jabber
12. jingle-jangle
13. knickknack
14. pitter-patter
15. riffraff
16. seesaw
17. splish-splash
18. ticktock
19. topsy-turvy
20. zigzag

Page 60:
1. bigwig
2. boohoo
3. bowwow
4. even-steven
5. claptrap
6. fuzzy-wuzzy
7. handy-dandy
8. heebie-jeebies
9. helter-skelter
10. hocus-pocus
11. hodgepodge

12. hoi polloi
13. hoity-toity
14. holy moly
15. hubbub
16. humdrum
17. itsy-bitsy, teeny-weeny
18. nitty-gritty
19. tutti-frutti
20. lovey-dovey

Page 61:
1. bat
2. ant
3. bear
4. bee
5. boar
6. dog
7. bull, lion
8. cat
9. cow
10. crow
11. cat
12. ape
13. owl
14. goat
15. gnu
16. pig
17. mice
18. cat
19. crab
20. rat
21. fish
22. pig
23. eel

Page 62:
1. b, 2. e, 3. c, 4. a, 5. d

Page 63:
1. d, 2. c, 3. b, 4. a, 5. e

Page 64:
1. e, 2. b, 3. c, 4. a, 5. d

Page 65:
1. does
2. excuse
3. suspect
4. buffet
5. produce
6. rebel
7. desert
8. read

Page 66:
1. present
2. object
3. moderate

4. contest
5. used
6. protest
7. wound
8. lead
9. polish, Polish
10. content

Page 67:
1. shower
2. refuse
3. incense
4. convict
5. Baton, baton
6. subject
7. drawer
8. minute
9. wind
10. insult

Page 68:
1. live
2. number
3. do
4. progress
5. row
6. separate
7. perfect
8. sewer
9. project
10. house

Page 69:
1. entrance
2. learned
3. sow
4. lives
5. dove
6. primer
7. putting
8. estimate
9. bow
10. Job, job

Page 70:
1. peaked
2. bass
3. permit
4. lima, Lima
5. tarry
6. Herb, herb
7. evening
8. record
9. tear
10. close

Page 71:
1. night, knight
2. fowl, foul
3. which, witch
4. sense, cents, scents
5. bawled, bald
6. to, two, too
7. meet, meat
8. ate, eight
9. threw, through
10. ceiling, sealing

Page 72:
1. sighed, side
2. hire, higher
3. herd, heard
4. Whether, weather
5. pair, pear
6. break, brake
7. bee, be
8. bear, bare
9. They're, there, their
10. haul, hall

Page 73:
1. Do, dew, due
2. know, no
3. maid, made
4. flu, flew, flue
5. cereal, serial
6. our, hour
7. flower, flour
8. lessen, lesson
9. die, dye
10. blew, blue

Page 74:
1. mail, male
2. miner, minor
3. dear, deer
4. feet, feat
5. pause, paws
6. weight, wait
7. whole, hole
8. tale, tail
9. steal, steel
10. rowed, rode, road

Page 75:
1. sees, seas
2. pail, pale
3. some, sum
4. desert, dessert
5. manors, manners
6. seen, scene
7. beach, beech
8. waist, waste
9. capital, capitol
10. sail, sale

Page 76:
1. Aye, I, eye
2. borough, burro, burrow
3. knew, new, gnu
4. raise, raze, rays
5. way, weigh, whey
6. cord, chord, cored
7. you, ewe, yew
8. rain, reign, rein
9. main, Maine, mane
10. four, Fore, for

Page 77:
1. pull
2. hit
3. tickle
4. strike
5. split
6. beat
7. carry
8. hold
9. jump
10. drive
11. climb
12. sling
13. play
14. scratch
15. run

Page 78:
1. bird
2. chickens
3. horse
4. cat
5. frog
6. dog
7. mouse
8. turkey
9. hen
10. fish

Page 79:
1. rat
2. bull
3. wolf, sheep
4. lamb
5. goose
6. possum
7. beaver
8. monkey
9. leopard
10. pigeon

Page 80:
1. crow
2. peacock
3. fly
4. hornet
5. butterflies

6. ants
7. snail
8. grasshopper
9. snake
10. bug

Page 81:
1. cap
2. pants
3. shirt
4. gloves
5. belt
6. collar
7. sleeve
8. shoestring
9. britches
10. shoe

Page 82:
1. blue
2. black
3. blue
4. red
5. blue
6. silver
7. red
8. green
9. pink
10. green
11. red
12. pink
13. red
14. red

Page 83:
1. apple
2. butter
3. cucumber
4. pie
5. egg
6. salt
7. cake
8. pickle
9. peas
10. fruitcake
11. pudding
12. beans
13. cookie
14. banana

Page 84:
1. #4, 2. #6, 3. #7, 4. #2,
5. #1, 6. #8, 7. #3, 8. #5,
9. #10, 10. #9

Page 85:
1. ears
2. thumbs
3. tongue
4. hand
5. blood
6. head
7. lip
8. lip
9. teeth
10. feet

Page 86:
1. nose, face
2. elbow
3. eyes, head
4. tooth, nail
5. chest
6. skin
7. hand, mouth
8. head, shoulders
9. head
10. head, heels
11. heart
12. throat

Page 87:
1. ear
2. nose
3. heels
4. hair
5. nose
6. head
7. nose
8. eyes
9. foot
10. finger
11. foot
12. neck

Page 88:
1. eyebrow
2. elbows
3. eye, eye
4. leg
5. eyes
6. neck
7. feet
8. tooth
9. tongue, cheek
10. heel
11. shoulder
12. head

Page 89:
1. Whoa!
2. Alas,
3. Mmm,
4. Aha!
5. Gosh,
6. Help!
7. Uh-oh,
8. Yuck!
9. Phew,
10. Ouch!

Page 90:
1. Hooray! We just won
the championships for
the first time in history!
2. Ooops, he just spilled a
little milk, but I won't cry
over it.
3. Eek! That's not a
rubber rat. It's a real one!
4. Darn, there's a hole in
my stocking.
5. Ugh! Somebody put
gooey green slime in my
sneakers!
6. Well, we have to feed
the rabbits before we
paint the kitchen.
7. Gee, it's almost 5
o'clock.
8. Bravo! You're the
greatest opera singer in
the world!
9. All right, class, let's
open our books to page
23.
10. Whoopee! I just found
the five dollars I was
looking for!

Page 91:
Answers will vary but
interjections should show
strong emotions for
sentences 1, 3, 6, 8, and
10 (and be punctuated
with exclamation marks.
Other interjections
should show milder
emotions (and be
followed by commas,
with periods at the end).

Page 92:
1. PER, TH, PL, TH
2. PL, PER, PER, ID, ID
3. PL, PL, PER, TH, TH,
TH
4. PER, TH, PL, PL, PL
5. PER, PER/TH,
PER/TH, PER/TH,
PER/TH
6. PER, TH, TH, TH, TH,
PL
7. PER, PL, ID, ID, ID
8. TH, TH, TH, TH, TH,
TH, PL
9. PL, PER, TH, PL
10. PL, TH, TH, PL, TH

Page 93:
1. S: singer, show, school;
P: songs, operas
2. S: man, rose;
P: flowers, daffodils
3. S: stick, butter, lemon,
flavor; P: eggs
4. S: shirt, belt,
toothbrush; P: socks,
handkerchiefs
5. S: street, ballpark;
P: blocks
6. S: book; P: stories,
students
7. S: monkey, zoo,
Chicago; P: peanuts,
cousins
8. S: circus; P: clowns,
noses, shoes, hats
9. S: teacher, boy, office,
principal; P: pencils
10. S: aquarium, friend,
whale, dad; P: sharks,
guppies

Page 94:
1. geese
2. women
3. deer
3. halves
5. teeth
6. alumni
7. mice
8. octopuses*
9. oxen
10. babies

*Sometimes the plural of
"octopus" is written as
"octopi" or "octopodes."
"Octopuses" is best.

Page 95:
1. C: cities, planet;
P: Earth, Rome,
Barcelona
2. C: mountains;
P: David, Everest,
Kilimanjaro
3. C: mom; P: Rachel's,
Taj Mahal, India, Masada,
Israel

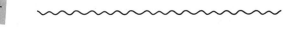

4. C: name, frog, name, rabbit; Gribbet, Hopper
5. C: magician, tricks; P: Houdini, Hungary
6. C: laptop, printer, cell; P: Apple, Brother, Nokia
7. C: woman, history; P: Harriet Tubman, America
8. C: river, world; P: Amazon, Nile

Page 96:
1. colony
2. shrewdness
3. hive
4. gang
5. herd
6. brood
7. pack
8. pace
9. skulk
10. gaggle
11. drift
12. kindle
13. barren
14. litter
15. warren
16. crash
17. trip
18. flock
19. knot
20. bale

Page 97:
1. neighbor
2. principal
3. snake
4. company
5. ringmaster
6. cousin
7. Dennis
8. friend
9. Isla
10. waitress

Page 98:
1. plays
2. ball
3. pie
4. plane
5. tests
6. meatballs
7. championship
8. Mount Rushmore
9. movies
10. home run

Page 99:
1. boredom
2. wisdom
3. equality
4. reality
5. permission
6. discussion
7. education
8. imagination
9. achiever
10. challenger
11. director
12. illustrator
13. tourist
14. finalist
15. attractiveness
16. business

Page 100:
buzzing, chirping, hooting, mooing, braying, oinking, bleating, baahing, clucking, gobbling, neighing, quacking, croaking, honking, trumpeting, roaring, howling, chattering, meowing, barking, squeaking

Page 101:
1. dad
2. mom
3. eye
4. kayak
5. noon
6. deed
7. bib
8. ma'am
9. level
10. did
11. nun
12. ewe
13. madam

Page 102:
1. toot
2. pup
3. peep
4. sis
5. Tut
6. radar
7. tot
8. rotor
9. solos
10. shahs
11. redder
12. reviver

Page 103:
1. #4, mad dam
2. #7, pit tip
3. #8, snug guns
4. #2, lap pal
5. #3, live evil
6. #10, won now
7. #9, swap paws
8. #6, pan nap
9. #5, pals slap
10. #1, bag gab

Page 104:
1. #9, pets step
2. #1, bad dab
3. #10, net ten
4. #4, cod doc
5. #5, gum mug
6. #3, sub bus
7. #6, star rats
8. #7, pat tap
9. #2, dog god
10. #8, straw warts

Page 105:
1. TRAGIC
2. OF GUM
3. HAM
4. I MOAN
5. LEMON
6. SIR
7. TAP
8. POOR DAN
9. MAYOR
10. BOOT

Page 106:
1. f, 2. c, 3. g, 4. h, 5. j
6. l, 7. a, 8. k, 9. d, 10. b,
11. e, 12. i

Page 107:
1. l, 2. c, 3. b, 4. d, 5. e,
6. a, 7. k, 8. i, 9. g, 10. f,
11. j, 12. h

Page 108:
1. l, 2. e, 3. f, 4. h, 5. b,
6. i, 7. j, 8. g, 9. c, 10. d,
11. k, 12.a

Page 109:
In order of their appearance in the story, the following words should be circled:
on, of, near, with, for, to, toward, with, under, down, to, along, behind, at, between, through, around, After, of, near, of, up, past, outside, of, with

Page 110:
1. **aboard** the good **ship**
2. **about** her **adventures**
3. **Above** our **heads**
4. **across** the **street**
5. **against** the **wall**
6. **After** an **hour**
7. **alongside** the **roadside**
8. **among** the neighborhood **cats**
9. **around** the noisy **jungle**
10. **at** the king's magnificent **palace**

Page 111:
1. T, 2. L, 3. D, 4. T, 5. D,
6. R, 7. T, 8. T, 9. T, 10. R

Page 112:
1. "**I** don't want to give her a lick of my lollipop," **he** shouted.
2. After the concert, **they** went back to their house for ice cream.
3. Once **she** was a princess, but now **she** sells gives haircuts to dogs.
4. **We** must remember to take the hamster with us on vacation or **it** will be lonely.
5. **You** must never forget that **we** rescued your duck from the stuck roller coaster.
6. **I** knew **they** wouldn't like it if **we** ate all their popcorn during the movie.
7. **He** and **she** used to speak Wu when **they** were little, but **they** forgot it.
8. **It** can't be true that **you** and **she** saw them wearing chicken costumes.
9. **He**'s so tall that his mother has to stand on a ladder to kiss him.

10. Right now **I**'m so tired **I** could sleep for a week at his house.

Page 113:
1. When she saw **him** dressed as a frog, she screamed, "Gribbit! Gribbit!"
2. They want **us** to go to the principal's office immediately.
3. Please call **them** and say that you can't dance the cha-cha-cha with **her** tonight.
4. If I told **you** once, I told **you** a million times, don't whistle while eating peanut butter.
5. She gave **me** the money, I put **it** in my sock, and I lost **it** in the dryer.
6. It broke down on the road and stranded **us** near Albuquerque
7. She beat **him** in the swim meet, but he beat **her** in the cooking contest.
8. You know that I want **you** to sing in the show, but they want **him**.
9. When you gave **it** to **him**, did he at least say, "Thank **you**"?
10. Serve **her** the cake, **him** the pie, **them** the cookies, and **us** the muffins.

Page 114:
1. **Her** dog tap dances while **his** hamster plays the piano. It's a cute act!
2. The directions say that **theirs** is the third house on the right.
3. I know that **my** mother won't let us do it, but let's ask anyway.
4. The truck lost **its** wheel going around the bend, and now it's stuck in the mud.
5. That's **mine**, not **yours**, so give it back!

6. They're painting **their** house with purple polka dots right over there.
7. **Hers** is a tale of bravery, heroism, and lollipops.
8. You're not going to take **your** toys and go home now, are you?
9. **Her** grandmother gave her a pet hippo for **her** birthday.
10. I'm ready to cook **his** recipe in **their** pots for **our** dinner.

Page 115:
Loraine and George had been friends since first grade. **She** was one month older than **he** was, but **he** was 4 inches taller than **she** was. **They** lived across the street from a beautiful park. "This park is **ours**," **she** once said. **She** liked to go to the park to read. **He** liked to go there to play ball. Then one day, **she** said to **him**, "I have a good idea for **us**. If **you** let **me** borrow **your** bat, **I** will let **you** read **my** favorite book."
"**It**'s a deal, **he** said. "**We** have lots of books at **our** house, but **I**'ve read **them** all."
"And **I** don't have a baseball bat at **my** house, so that's why **I** have to borrow **yours**."
Their idea was a good one, and **they** had a perfect day. **Hers** was a good book, and **she** played ball with **his** bat. **They** were quite happy with the switch **they** had made.

Page 116:
1. My, its
2. her, my
3. them, it
4. ours, theirs
5. He, her, It, its
6. I, it
7. He, she, it, she, she, it

8. Our, its, my
9. you, it, them, I, you
10. Her, your him

Page 117:
It was Jen's first day of school. **She** jumped out of **her** bed and took a fast shower. **She** then looked in **her** mirror and said to **her**self, "I look great today." Then **she** ate **her** breakfast, picked up **her** backpack, kissed **her** mother and father, and waved goodbye to **them** as **she** flew out the door. On the way to **her** school, **she** met **her** next-door neighbor, Tim. "Hi, Tim," **she** called to **him**. "Can **we** walk to school together?"
"Sure," **he** said. Then **he** asked, "Would **you** like **me** to carry **your** backpack?"
She answered, "No thanks. **I** can do it **my**self."
And off **they** went, carrying **their** own backpacks to school.
"Lucky **us**," **he** said.
"Why are **we** so lucky?" **she** asked.
"Because **we** go to such a great school. **We** have great teachers. And even the food in **our** cafeteria is great."
"**You**'re right," **she** said. "**We** are lucky."

Page 118:
1. My name is Baron Egbert von Loopingdorf Schitzelheim Gruffingmerz, III.
2. The volcano has erupted and hot, molten lava is rushing down the mountainside toward the village!
3. I saw the biggest movie star in the world at the mall. (or !)

4. Math class is next.
5. At what temperature does water freeze?
6. There's no school today because of the snowstorm. (or !)
7. Many people think that the biggest tree in the world is in Santa Maria del Tule, a small town in the state of Oaxaca, Mexico.
8. I hate peanut butter and broccoli sandwiches. (or !)
9. Are you the boy who rescued the gerbils from the cat?
10. The giant model of tyrannosaurus rex has come alive!
11. Is the Statue of Liberty in New York or New Jersey?
12. Run for the hills!

Page 119:
1. In 1897, 13 years before he died, Mark Twain pronounced, **"**The report of my death was an exaggeration.**"**
2. One of the best American singers ever, Marian Anderson, wisely said, **"**Everyone has a gift for something, even if it is the gift of being a good friend.**"**
3. Charles Dickens must have read a lot of bad books because he once stated, **"**There are books of which the backs and covers are by far the best parts.**"**
4. Ben Franklin, who accomplished a lot in his life, gave pretty good advice when he said, **"**Early to bed and early to rise, makes a man healthy, wealthy, and wise.**"**
5. Albert Einstein must have known what he was talking about when he advised, **"**Anyone who has never made a mistake has never tried

anything new."
6. Although she was definitely a somebody, it's strange that the great American poet of the 1800s, Emily Dickinson, once asked, "I'm nobody! Who are you?"
7. Thomas Jefferson uttered something worth thinking about he observed, "I find that the harder I work, the more luck I seem to have."
8. Singer, actress, writer, and activist Maya Angelou once declared, "How important it is for us to recognize and celebrate our heroes and she-roes!"

Page 120:
1. "What ingredients did you put in this fabulous stew?" Alberto asked the new chef.
2. "Four score and seven years ago," said Abraham Lincoln at the beginning of his Gettysburg Address.
3. "Make sure the baby is in bed by eight o'clock," Mrs. Youngman instructed the babysitter.
4. "Class, today's big test has been cancelled because of a shortage of sharpened pencils," stated the professor with a sigh.
5. "Don't bite down!" screamed the hysterical dentist with his finger still in the patient's mouth.
6. "Which river carries the greatest volume of water, the Amazon or the Nile?" asked the geography teacher.
7. "Who did this?" wondered my aunt in her soft, but quizzical, voice.

8. "The Statue of Liberty was brought across the Atlantic Ocean by ship from France in 350 pieces in 1885," stated the brochure.

Page 121:
1. "I never wear orange hats," said the movie star, "because orange doesn't go well with my hazel eyes."
2. "When you add salt to this soup," instructed the cooking teacher, "just a pinch will do."
3. "Thanks for getting me that DVD for my birthday," said his grandson, "because science-fiction horror movies are my favorites."
4. "You're playing left field today," called the coach, "and make sure you keep your head up during the game."
5. "How can you study for your history test," asked her mother, "with the music turn up so high?"
6. "Hurry and turn on the TV," shouted my aunt as she ran into the room, "because Uncle Harry's being interviewed on the news!"
7. "I used to know the names of all the highest mountains," said my friend, "but I can't remember them now."
8. "Are you going to the same camp this summer," asked the girl behind me in line, "or a new one?"

Page 122:
1. The teacher asked, "Does anyone know if Jászalsószentgyörgy is in Poland or Hungary?"
2. "The Tyrannosaurus rex is loose!" cried the zookeeper frantically.

3. "I know what the secret of Goo La La is," she whispered softly, "but I'm never going to reveal it."
4. The big sign at the front door stated simply, "Step into the haunted house on your right foot first."
5. "President William Howard Taft kept a cow on the White House lawn," the famous historian said, "and she slept in the garage."
6. She whispered, "A tomato is really a fruit," and disappeared into the bushes.
7. "Why did you wear your pants on your head?" asked his mother calmly.
8. My neighbor yelled from across the street, "Turn down that music because the noise is driving me crazy!"
9. "My name is Loraine," she explained, "but I spell it with only one r in the middle."
10. "I won the election at last!" exclaimed the jubilant candidate.

Page 123:
1. To Jennifer, Timothy was the best singer in the world.
2. After the broken roller coaster shut down, down came the repairmen from the top level.
3. At the supermarket I bought peanut butter, apple pie, ice cream, and corn flakes.
4. The king walked in, in his royal robes.
5. For my pets I always have a supply of kitty litter, chewy bones, flea spray, and bird seed.
6. When the monsters came out, out ran the frightened kid.

7. In the costume department you'll find suits of armor, witches' hats, soldiers' uniforms, and wedding gowns.
8. The dancer twirled on, on her new dancing shoes.
9. At my drug store I sell baby powder, razor blades, hand lotion, and electric toothbrushes.
10. When the rocket shot up, up went all our eyes to follow it.

Page 124:
1. For the picnic she packed a blanket, bug spray, cheese sandwiches, plastic cups, and iced tea.
2. For Mrs. Thomas, Richard will be the best person to cut her hair.
3. As the dark storm clouds gathered above, above our heads we heard the sound of thunder.
4. A few minutes after, the thunderstorm came.
5. Before the crowd drew near, near the speaker a microphone was placed.
6. For Halloween, I wore a mask fashioned from colored paper and chicken feathers, a blouse created from an old pillowcase, a skirt made from neckties, and boots that were really big plastic bottles.
7. Even though her best friend is Mary, Jane voted for Susie in the election.
8. After the plane flew over, over at the airport the people cheered.
9. Just the day before, the Broadway show opened.
10. At college my brother studies American history, French literature, Egyptian hieroglyphics, and Chinese cooking.

Page 125:
1. clown, gown, town, down, frown
2. goat, wrote, note, boat, coat, float
3. Lou, zoo, glue, shoe, gnu, true
4. Chuck, truck, stuck, duck, luck, Chuck
5. Rose, blows, nose, toes, clothes, goes
6. ghost, host, roast, toast, boast, most

Page 126:
1. bitter, freezing, critter, sneezing
2. head, white, red, height
3. ball, cheering, wall, hearing
4. bowl, tasty, soul, pasty
5. mop, breaks, shop, cakes
6. mow, grooming, grow, blooming

Page 127:
Student poems will vary.

Page 128:
Student poems will vary.

Page 129:
1. matches
2. tigers
3. eyelashes
4. classes
5. medals
6. marches, torches
7. boxes
8. breakfasts
9. atlases
10. crutches

Page 130:
1. taxes
2. witches
3. computers
4. compasses
5. metropolises
6. flashes
7. prefixes
8. scratches
9. leashes
10. skyscrapers

Page 131:
1. birthdays
2. countries
3. decoys
4. cavities
5. chimneys
6. agencies
7. alleys
8. blueberries
9. buys
10. batteries

Page 132:
1. children
2. geese
3. mice
4. oxen
5. teeth
6. feet
7. women
8. shelves
9. deer
10. alumni
Challenge: (sample) sheep

Page 133:
1. ancient, species
2. scientists, weird
3. foreign, either
4. sufficient, leisure
5. seismologist, financier
6. forfeit, their
7. Caffeine, protein
8. height
9. seized, kaleidoscope
10. society, efficiently

Page 134:
1. **wr**eck, **p**sychologist, **wr**ist, **kn**ee, **kn**uckles
2. **gn**u, **gn**awed
3. **wr**etched, **p**sychiatrist, **p**tomaine, **wr**ong, **p**neumonia
4. **gn**ome, **kn**ob, **kn**ight
5. **wr**ap, **wr**en, **wr**iggle, **kn**ock
6. **wr**estle, **wr**inkle
7. **p**sychic, **kn**ew, **kn**ife, **kn**ap-sack
8. **wr**ote, **kn**ead
9. **kn**itted, **p**terodactyl
10. **gn**ash, **kn**ot, **wr**ing

Page 135:
1. plum**b**er, **w**ho, Conne**c**ticut, climb**e**d

2. We**d**nesday, han**d**some, han**d**kerchief
3. T**h**omas, r**h**ymed, **gh**ost
4. Lincol**n**, solem**n**, hym**n**, Illinois, Christmas
5. ras**p**berry, cup**b**oard, is**l**and, Arkansa**s**
6. Listen, g**u**ard, ba**d**ge, cas**t**le, tal**k**, fol**k**
7. si**gn**, colum**n**, buil**d**ing, ais**l**e
8. bis**c**uit, g**u**itar, fas**t**en, lat**c**h, ans**w**er
9. but**c**her, si**gh**ed, **w**hen, g**u**ilty, g**u**est, hal**f**, yol**k**
10. **W**here, ca**l**m, ca**l**f, lam**b**, is**l**e, pa**l**m, debri**s**

Page 136:
1. capable, acceptable, illegible, possible
2. courageous, ferocious
3. sist**er**, danc**er**, sing**er**, act**or**
4. attention, election, explosion, celebration
5. terrible, horrible, deplorable, unbelievable, inexcusable
6. hideous, gorgeous, furious, mysterious, malicious, courteous
7. may**or**, govern**or**, ambassad**or**, swimm**er**, winn**er**, riv**er**
8. permission, television, discussion, mansion
9. superstitious, invisible, professor, miserable, discussion, aviator's, glorious, incredible
10. illusion, rumor, abominable, audible, expedition

Page 137:
deplorable
Challenge: (sample) great

Page 138:
minuscule
Challenge: (sample) huge

Page 139:
melancholy
Challenge: (sample) exultant

Page 140:
grotesque
Challenge: (sample) prepossessing

Page 141:
obtuse
Challenge: (sample) gifted

Page 142:
hygienic
Challenge: (sample) unhygienic

Page 143:
pusillanimous
Challenge: (sample) bold

Page 144:
1. soothing
2. disagreeable
3. lovely
4. genuine
5. dexterous
6. simple
7. truthful
8. malodorous
9. trivial
10. petite
11. fascinating
12. celebrated
13. meritorious
14. artificial
15. cautious
16. trustworthy
17. opaque
18. tranquil
19. inquisitive
20. delectable

Page 145:
1. youthful
2. virtuous
3. tame
4. docile
5. ordinary
6. svelte
7. industrious
8. compassionate
9. handsome
10. genteel

Page 146:
1. affable
2. robust
3. generous
4. sagacious
5. affluent

6. cautious
7. peaceable
8. humble
9. frugal
10. modest

Page 147:
1. valuable
2. fragrant
3. solid
4. attractive
5. fascinating
6. portable
7. melodious
8. faultless
9. newfangled
10. sharp

Page 148:
1. whispered
2. shouted
3. announced
4. mumbled
5. growled
6. wondered
7. sobbed
8. giggled
9. pleaded
10. gasped

Page 149:
1. barked
2. sighed
3. declared
4. blubbered
5. hissed
6. inquired
7. begged
8. chuckled
9. protested
10. threatened

Page 150:
1. teased
2. cheered
3. demanded
4. reported
5. fumed
6. asked
7. beseeched
8. whined
9. argued
10. urged

Page 151:
1. S, 2. A, 3. S, 4. S, 5. A,
6. S, 7. A, 8. A, 9. S, 10. A

Page 152:
1. A, 2. S, 3. A, 4. A, 5. A,
6. S, 7. S, 8. A, 9. S, 10. S

Page 153:
1. S, 2. A, 3. S, 4. S, 5. S,
6. A, 7. S, 8. S, 9. A, 10. A

Page 154:
1. A, 2. A, 3. S, 4. A, 5. S,
6. S, 7. A, 8. S, 9. A, 10. S

Page 155:
1. rash
2. rational
3. thwart
4. assiduous
5. vile
6. constantly
7. maladroit
8. confuse
9. diffident
10. radiant

Page 156:
1. exonerate
2. heal
3. prolixity
4. misery
5. timid
6. fondness
7. awake
8. expand
9. indifferent
10. ineffective

Page 157:
1. gripping
2. salubrious
3. insolent
4. comfortable
5. luscious
6. benevolent
7. sagacious
8. unruly
9. clamorous
10. bucolic

Page 158:
1. outstanding
2. iniquitous
3. minuscule
4. gargantuan
5. euphoric
6. disconsolate
7. accelerated
8. sluggardly
9. percipient
10. scorching

Page 159:
1. gallop
2. hop
3. waddle
4. squirm
5. slither
6. soar
7. burrow
8. swim
9. swing
10. dive
11. crawl
12. climb
13. swoop
14. jump
15. run

Page 160:
1. chose
2. did
3. ate
4. got
5. knew
6. left
7. lost
8. met
9. paid
10. rose
11. ran
12. saw
13. sat
14. slid
15. took

Page 161:
1. took
2. bit
3. broke
4. came
5. wrote
6. drew
7. shook
8. froze
9. swam
10. slid

Page 162:
1. wore
2. told
3. strove
4. spoke
5. shot
6. rose
7. lost
8. grew
9. drove
10. bound

Page 163:
1. bought
2. fought
3. caught
4. brought
5. taught
6. sought
7. thought
8. bought
9. brought
10. thought

Page 164:
1. stung
2. sprang
3. clung
4. flung
5. rang
6. wrung
7. brought
8. sang

Page 165:
The following verbs
should be circled:
burst, beat, cut, set, rid.
Challenge: go, went

Page 166:
1. ate, eight
2. blew, blue
3. flew, flu, flue
4. knew, gnu
5. read, red
6. rode, rowed, road
7. wrung, rung
8. told, tolled
9. threw, through
10. wrote, rote